## Praise for Jace Carlton and *Breaking the Stillness*

Jace Carlton's latest book, *Breaking the Stillness*, is exquisite!

I loved how raw and vulnerable his writing is, and he doesn't hold back his emotions that may seem hard to translate on paper. I loved feeling the emotions and thoughts of what Jace was experiencing, and the internal struggles and the journey he takes the reader on. His style of writing gave me a small peek into Jace's own wilderness journeys and life experiences!

Something else I loved about *Breaking the Stillness* was the section at the end of the book where Jace shares what inspired certain poems and songs he's written. The reader gets to "peek behind the curtain", to see where the inspiration comes from and how the magic happens.

*Breaking the Stillness*, is truly a gift. It transforms you toward the end to see the world a little bit brighter, that even on the hard days things will work out and experience can be a hard teacher. However, the experiences we have will transform us into who we are meant to become.

*Breaking the Stillness* is truly a wonderful journey!

— **Laurel Christiansen**

*Breaking the Stillness* is a masterpiece, and I am forever thankful for having read it. Jace's mastery of the art in telling life and loving has pulled long lost memories from my youth. Many brought some knowing chuckles, and yes, even a few tears.

I can see a lot of the influence of Rod McKuen in *Breaking the Stillness*. Many, many thanks to Jace for his willingness to be so vulnerable. It helps those of us who find it too difficult to express what's in our own hearts.

— **Bruce Sexton**

It's clear to me that *Breaking the Stillness* was written with warmth and love. SO many of my long forgotten memories, both wonderful and even the not so wonderful, came flooding back so gloriously as I read these pages! It made me wonder how he could have known and written so perfectly about them!

I'm sure you'll find memories of your own come to life, and if you didn't have the words to express what was in your heart then, you certainly will now!

Jace's poems and songs tell *our* stories, from the pain and sadness of heartbreak and loss to the pure joy of true love and every stop in between.

Take the journey and rediscover the power of love!

— **Debra Hunter Miller**


It is extraordinarily personal and wonderful! Several of the poems caused a bit of an eye leak. Since I have a love of the beach and seashore, I found those poems especially wonderful.

— **Kate Kruley**


It's perfect! I absolutely love it!

— **Linda Foss**

*Breaking the Stillness* is a sweet sampling of writings which will both satisfy and leave the reader craving more. It is a unique keyhole look into a young man's quest for love, companionship, and understanding.

As a songwriter, I particularly enjoyed reading the story behind many of Jace's poems and songs. It fascinates me to see where other writer's inspiration comes from and helps me to strengthen my own awareness of what and who is around me, either now or in my memories.

— **Carmen Bennett**

Wow! Wow! *Breaking the Stillness* is a winner! Jace has taken me back to a place of remembrance, and has allowed me to see how much I have grown from what I experienced. He is an amazing writer who leaves you holding on to your seat and to keep reading to the finish!

A fan forever!

— **Cindy Blake**

It was such a beautiful and enjoyable journey from start to finish that played a symphony of emotions in my heart.

— **Janet Vargas**

Oh, my heart! *Breaking the Stillness* is breathtakingly romantic!

— **Pamela Sue Knightson**

# BREAKING THE STILLNESS

# BREAKING THE STILLNESS

## JACE CARLTON

1423
PRESS
Eagle Mountain, Utah

*Other Books by Jace Carlton*

**Novels**
The Reunion

**Poetry**
Sounds of Darkness

**Private Edition**
Reflections

*Breaking the Stillness*
By Jace Carlton

Published by 1423 Press
212 E. Crossroads Blvd, #184
Saratoga Springs, UT 84045

Copyright © 2020 Jace Carlton

Without limiting the rights under copyright reserved above, no part of this publication may be reproduced, stored in or introduced into a retrieval system, or transmitted, in any form, or by any means (electronic, mechanical, photocopying, recording, or otherwise), without the prior written permission of both copyright owner and the above publisher of this book; except by a reviewer, who may quote brief passages in a review to be printed in a magazine or newspaper, either electronic, print, or both. For permissions please contact 1423 Press at the address above.

"Sounds of Darkness", "In Need of You", "Going, Going …", "Give Me a Second Chance", "Towel", "Heavy Clouds of Rain", "Once", "Please Write", "Cold", "3 a.m.", "Do You Still Love Me?", "Caution: One Way", "I'm Only Me", "Someone Special", "UXR 324", "9:14 Illinois Central", and "Hello …" are from *Sounds of Darkness*, published by Diamond Heights Press, copyright © 1976 by Jace Carlton

Excerpt from *At First Glance* copyright © 2020 by Jace Carlton
Excerpt from *Second Chance* copyright © 2020 by Jace Carlton

Edited by Terrie Dailey Morgan
1423 Press Logo by Brianna Rawlings, Fiverr.com/braidedlady
Cover Photography by Jordan Steranka on Unsplash
Cover and Book Design by James Woosley, FreeAgentPress.com

First Printing, October 2020

ISBN: 978-0-9996855-4-9 (hardcover)
ISBN: 978-0-9996855-5-6 (paperback)
ISBN: 978-0-9996855-6-3 (eBook)
ISBN: 978-0-9996855-7-0 (Kindle)

Library of Congress Control Number: 2020913117

The Lighthouse logo is a trademark of 1423 Press.

# Contents

| | |
|---|---|
| Acknowledgments | xv |
| Dedication | xvii |
| Author's Note | xix |

## Searching — 1

| | |
|---|---|
| Searching | 5 |
| Sounds of Darkness | 6 |
| In Need of You | 8 |
| Heavy Clouds of Rain | 9 |
| Christmas, 1969 | 10 |
| Towel | 11 |
| Going, Going … | 12 |
| Give Me a Second Chance | 13 |
| Once | 14 |
| Please Write | 16 |
| Cold | 17 |
| Lost | 18 |
| Lost, 2 | 19 |
| 3 a.m. | 20 |
| Do You Still Love Me? | 21 |
| Caution: One Way | 22 |
| Somehow | 23 |
| I'm Only Me | 25 |

## Longing — 27

| | |
|---|---|
| Someone Special | 31 |
| UXR 324 | 32 |
| 9:14 Illinois Central | 33 |
| Beach, 4 a.m. | 34 |
| Beach, 6 p.m. | 35 |

## Hopeful 37
- Hello … 41
- Sanctuary 42
- Angel in the Dark 44
- Clinging to Love 45
- November 46
- December 47
- The Day Spring Came 48
- Timberline 49
- Spring 51
- Softly 52
- Time Piece 54
- Surf and Stars 55
- Love, 1 56
- Love, 2 57
- Love, 3 58
- Juliet 59
- Two Hearts Are One 60
- Coming Together … Again 62
- Misty Clouds 63
- Dreams 64
- Something Happened to Me on the Way to the Moon 65
- Silhouette 66

## Songs 69
- Lovin' You 73
- No One to Remember Your Name 75
- In My Memory 77
- The One 79
- If We Ever Love Again 81
- Eternally 83
- Crossroads 85
- The Edge of Forever and Goodbye 87
- A Place for Her Piano 90
- Another Lonely New Year's Eve 93
- Right Here Waiting 96

| | |
|---|---|
| BEHIND THE MUSE | 99 |
|    My Muse, the Stories, and other things | 101 |
|    Christmas, 1969 | 103 |
|    Towel | 103 |
|    Please Write | 104 |
|    I'm Only Me | 106 |
|    UXR 324 | 107 |
|    Hello … | 110 |
|    Sanctuary | 111 |
|    Clinging to Love | 111 |
|    Timberline | 114 |
|    Softly | 120 |
|    Love, 2 | 121 |
|    Juliet | 122 |
|    Two Hearts Are One | 123 |
|    Silhouette | 123 |
|    The One | 124 |
|    If We Ever Love Again | 124 |
|    Eternally | 125 |
|    The Edge of Forever and Goodbye | 126 |
|    A Place for Her Piano | 127 |
|    Another Lonely New Year's Eve | 127 |
|    Right Here Waiting | 128 |
|    Old Songs | 129 |
| THE END (ALMOST) | 133 |
|    (We'll Always Go There ) Together | 137 |
| THE END | 141 |
|    Childhood Dreams | 142 |
| SOME FINAL THOUGHTS | 145 |
| ABOUT THE AUTHOR | 149 |
| SPECIAL EXCERPT OF *AT FIRST GLANCE* | 155 |
| SNEAK PEEK OF *SECOND CHANCE* | 161 |
|    Missing | 165 |

# Acknowledgments

**For my wife, Kathi, because** it all begins with love at home. You've been an angel as I've so often drifted into memories to create my poems, songs, and books. Your love allows me to soar!

For Terrie Dailey Morgan, my editor extraordinaire! You do so much to take what I write to that next level, and I'm so grateful for your talent and desire to always have my back.

For James Woosley of Free Agent Press. Your layout and design of my books and covers is simply the best! You did such an *amazing* job with my novel, *The Reunion*, and I'm so grateful to have you on my team for many more books to come!

For Laurel Christiansen, Pamela Sue Knighton, Alison Ratliff, Dawn Dufault Williams, Elise Glover Page, McKensie Ocana, Bruce Sexton, Debra Hunter Miller, Kate Kruley, Carmen Bennett, Tammy Herring, Janet Roberts Mullen, Cindy Blake, Janet Vargas, Rica Van Katwyk, Elizabeth Williams-Starke, and Linda McGrath Foss for reading the initial manuscript and offering your very helpful suggestions and comments. Thank you for making *Breaking the Stillness* better than I ever imagined it could be!

For Lou Lois, friend and comrade in arms. This journey into publishing would never have begun so many years ago without your encouraging words and persistent prodding. Thanks for believing in me, even before I believed in myself.

For Caren, my sweet, loving cousin. Over these last few years you've become the younger sister I never had. Your amazing support and loving encouragement (not to mention our chats where we can't stop laughing!!) go way beyond what words can describe. Love you, Boo! 10 … 9 … 8 ……..

Finally, for each of you who have read my books and have supported my writing over the years with your cards and letters and coming to my book signings! Your encouragement means everything to me, and your comments are always such a joy to receive! I can't wait to share *more* books with you that are in various stages of development!

# Dedication

For you.

You who are broken hearted.

You who are searching, longing, and hoping for a forever love.
Never give up on your quest! It may be hard,
it may even seem impossible or terribly frightening,
but in the end it is SO worth it! Keep trying!!!

You who are blissful lovers.

And also to you who are somewhere in between.
I know so well how it feels to be in limbo,
your heart neither soaring nor shattered,
your emotions have recovered from the last time,
but you're not quite ready for the next time.

If any one of these poems or songs resonates within you, then
I will be happy. For then we will have shared a bit of love and
friendship … even if it was from a distance.

Finally … for Caren.

# Author's Note

**A FUNNY THING HAPPENED ON** my way to a law degree … I wrote and published a book of poetry! After that, I realized that creativity, in some form or another, was what I *really* wanted, nay *needed*, to do as a career. I haven't always followed that path, but when I have I've been true to myself and to my heart. That brings an inner peace that's difficult for me to find anywhere else.

I wrote my first poems when I was 13 years old because I was in love and I wanted to impress my first girlfriend. It worked! But all I knew of poetry at that time was the kind of poems I read in books my parents had on their bookshelves such as "Best Loved American Poets" and "Most Loved British Poets of All Time." Those, and other similar books, gave me the impression that poetry was all about rhyme and rhythm, so that's how I wrote my poems. Now, that was fine to begin with, and it certainly paid off a year later after I'd bought my first guitar and started writing songs, but there was just something unsettling to me about continuing to write my poems in that way. It just didn't feel natural, so I set my poems aside and carried on with my songwriting.

A few years later I tried again for a short time when I met a very special girl while studying and traveling in Europe (what is it about falling in love with a girl that makes a guy wax poetic?!). After returning home, the cards and letters we shared back and forth (and an occasional poem) continued for a while, but eventually they, and my writing, faded away.

However, a year later I discovered a new way to express my heart through poetry, as I discovered the writings of Rod McKuen who wrote in a more "free verse" style. I was *so* excited about this discovery, and from that point on I have written my poems in that style as you'll discover in these pages.

Initially, I never intended to ever allow my writings to see the light of day as I felt they were too personal. Writing for a girlfriend was one thing, but beyond that? Not a chance! I wrote because I wanted to preserve the moment. It wasn't to impress anyone (other than those aforementioned girlfriends), but rather to capture a feeling or an emotion and get it down on paper to be savored at a later time. However, years later, after sharing some of my poems with a few of my very closest friends, I was encouraged to "put them out there!" Hesitantly, I did so, and I was humbled and blessed by the heartfelt accolades my work received.

I've been asked if I have a favorite place that I like to write, and I once had an apartment with a bay window that my desk fit into perfectly. Since I've always felt my best writing is done at night I could sit at my desk and look out over the city lights. I've also spent many days and nights at the seashore, alone. However, when an idea or inspiration strikes I write it down immediately before it's lost, no matter where I am. (Just ask my wife about the times I've reached for my pocket notebook in the middle of watching a movie, or the time I did so during a Kenny Loggins concert years ago!) If I don't have my notebook with me, a scrap of paper or a napkin will become my original manuscript. One night, when I was 19, I was at a dance when inspiration hit and the only thing I could find to write on was a paper tablecloth. When I was done I took the whole tablecloth home, even though my poem didn't take up more than a square foot area (and it's still in my filing cabinet). At some later time I took those scraps of paper, napkins, (and yes, paper tablecloths) and refined and reworked them into their finished forms. Very sadly, at some point during one of many moves in the mid to late 70s, I lost a thick binder of over seventy five of my original poems and songs. Searching high and low for weeks, and trying my best to remember where the last time was that I held that binder in my hands still didn't help. Gone forever. It's one of life's mysteries.

The first book of poetry I ever published was a book titled *Sounds of Darkness*. The year was 1976. Family and friends loved it, and it sold well in a variety of bookstore chains and independent bookstores throughout the greater San Francisco Bay Area (basically Santa Rosa to San Jose), and thanks to one of my older brothers, a few chain bookstores in Southern California also carried it with very positive results.

However, I was especially grateful for the cards and letters I received from strangers, because *then* I knew that my poems were reaching beyond just my family and friends, and to others whose hearts my writings were touching as I had hoped.

*Breaking the Stillness* is a compilation of my favorite poems from *Sounds of Darkness*, my second (and unpublished) manuscript, *Rainwater Tapestry*, and my third (unpublished) manuscript which shares its title with this book.

Over the years I've also enjoyed writing song lyrics, and some of my favorites are also included in this book. I'm always looking for collaborators to assist me in making my lyrics come to life (with the exception of *The Edge of Forever and Goodbye,* which has already been recorded). If you are so moved, you may reach me through my publisher.

Nearly all of these poems were written between the ages of 20 and 25, so if a word or phrase might seem a bit out of date to you, that's why. You're getting the complete, unedited version of these poems. As for the lyrics, for the most part they were written within the last 23 years, during which time I spent 8 years in the music industry in Nashville.

One final note ... over the years I've been asked what inspired some of my poems and lyrics, and when I've done book signings or taught creative writing classes I've been more than happy to share some of those stories. Now, with the publication of *Breaking the Stillness*, I'm sharing some of those stories with you here as well. You'll find a star (★) next to their titles, and you'll find their stories in a special section at the back of the book.

Jace Carlton
April 23, 2020

# Searching

Somewhere someone is reaching out
looking for a hand to hold
to help them through today,
searching for a ray of hope
to light their way,
saying a prayer that somewhere
someone will hear their cry.

Somewhere someone is reaching out
for you.

*Jace Carlton*

**WE SEARCH ... FOR MONTHS,** years, sometimes even a lifetime to find one love, one heart, one person that we can love, and who will love us in return with the kind of love we so desperately desire to share. To love purely, to love unconditionally, to love forever. But what is *forever*?

For some, forever is endless ... no end to time or space. Eternal!

For others, forever is the ultimate bliss ... joy going on and on!

For still others, forever may also mean endless pain after a loss.

What is forever to you?

# SEARCHING

I've been searching for you forever.
Is there a chance you might be near?

I've looked everywhere …
    empty rooms,
    busy streets,
    along too many beaches to count,
    through misty forests,
    and while hitchhiking through
        mountain passes,
        big cities,
        and small country villages.

I know someday I'll find you.
    I hope.
But your eyes elude me.

I'll know you by your eyes,
for in them I'll see the love I've been searching for …
    forever.

## SOUNDS OF DARKNESS

It's quiet on the beach tonight.
Fires burn as young lovers
      sit close to each other
    trying to keep warm.
A wave washed a bottle up to the shore,
but before I could reach it
another wave washed it back.
Maybe there was a note in it
that I'll never have the chance to answer.

It's quiet.
The sky with no clouds.
The beach with no rocks
      for the surf to crash into.
Even the lovers are quiet,
doing their talking in silent thoughts,
not needing spoken words
    to say what they feel.

*Breaking the Stillness*

It's quiet.
No birds. No cars passing
     on the nearby highway.
The only thing you can hear
    are the sounds of darkness.
The night sounds.
The empty sounds.
They're empty
     since you're not with me.

It's quiet …
and without you
     the stillness is heavy.
Only a wave …
washing up
another bottle to the shore …
         breaks the stillness.

*Jace Carlton*

# IN NEED OF YOU

The phone rings
      and my call goes unanswered.
The minutes I hang on
waiting for you to answer
seem like hours.
I keep calling back
hoping you'd arrived in between ...
      since the last.
Each time I let it ring longer,
perhaps hoping to catch you
      just coming in,
           or ... before going out again.
But each time
the wait is lonelier.
It seems like the times
      when I need you the most ...

         you're not there.

# HEAVY CLOUDS OF RAIN

Open doors, empty chairs,
dirty footprints on ice-cold stairs.
The pictures hang crooked
      on dusty walls.
Your fading footsteps
      haunt the halls
           of my mind.

As I look out my window
    as the night begins to fall
I see heavy clouds of rain.
Approaching silently, but swiftly,
they fill my head and block out
      the sun that once was there
          with your love.

# CHRISTMAS, 1969 ★

Emptiness.




                                                        Hope.

# TOWEL ★

You excused yourself from me
on the beach that day
and walked back to the house
to wash and clean up.
I soon followed,
        but it wasn't soon enough.
You were gone.

You left me behind
with a house full of our memories ...
photos of us,
        my favorite photo of you,
pieces of driftwood you'd selected just for me,
and probably the last thing you touched ...
        something for me to save
with the rest of our memories in our special box ...

        hanging from a rack in the bathroom ...

              a sandy towel.

## GOING, GOING ...

Quiet.

Don't say it.  You don't have to.
I know.

I knew when you weren't looking.
I knew when you weren't talking.
I knew when you didn't see
       how I've broken up inside.
I knew then
so please don't say anything now.
I know ...
       I understand.

Or at least ... I'm trying.

*Breaking the Stillness*

# GIVE ME A SECOND CHANCE

After we've had a fight
don't walk past me
      and ignore me.

Don't hate me
    for something I've said or done.
Touch me
      and show me you still care.

But only if you really do.

## ONCE

You walk away
as I watch from the window.
The sound of your footsteps,
      now growing fainter,
as the heavy beating of my heart
      screams in my ears.
I thought maybe this time
we would make it,
but you can see as easily as I do
where we stand now ...
           far apart.

Once we laughed.
Once we loved.
Once we lived as one.
But that was once some time ago,
when there was a warm sun
and walks along the beach
and horseback riding in the country.

*Breaking the Stillness*

Falling now are the autumn leaves,
beautiful in their
       multicolored variation,
but still dead.
Covering up the path we walked.
Waiting for the winter snow
    to come and bury it
until a bright spring sun can melt the snow,
exposing a fresh path
      for new lovers to walk.
And come summer
their path will change to one
    along the beach.

Maybe the seasons
    will be good to them
like they were for us
       for a short time ...
           once.

*Jace Carlton*

# PLEASE WRITE ★

Could you see me now
    if you tried?
You've been away for so long
do you even remember
      what I look like?

When you left I said
    "See ya later!"
        and prayed.
You said "Good-bye."
      Did you mean it?

I sit here,
    right here,
        day after day,
writing long love letters to you.
Some are never sent
    because you once said
you didn't like the mushy kind.
Of the ones that do find their way
      into the nearest mail box
few are ever answered.

I lie awake each night and wonder
    if you're just so very busy ...
        or whether you just don't care.

I really wish I knew.

# COLD

I picture you near me,
though you're so far away.
The nights are cold
and days so lonely.

Empty can't explain how I feel.
Since you left
I can't get anything right.
I want to make amends
but you won't listen.
I won't force you to come back to me
      or even to listen,
but …
      won't you just give me a chance?

# LOST

We were so in love once, remember?
And it wasn't so long ago
that I held you in my arms
and told you how much I loved you
    and how much I wanted you ...
        and, oh ... how much I needed you.

I hold your picture in my hands,
    it's the closest I can be to you now,
and try, somehow, to move past
        this shattered heart.
Missing you this way ...
    it's more than I can bear.

Remember the shops of Sausalito and Carmel?
Remember the cable car ride,
and the night we were alone
    in that glass elevator heading to the stars
        with a full moon and a clear sky?
Remember our late night walks along the beach?
Remember the dreams we made together?

Do you remember us at all?

# LOST, 2

I walk through the room
and the emptiness
echoes off the walls.
The fire in the fireplace crackles
and shadows flicker on the ceiling.
My thoughts wander aimlessly,
my life feels so useless,
my dreams so futile
since you've walked out of my life.

# 3 A.M.

Heavy rain
blows against the window
        by a bitter wind.
The light from the crackling fireplace
creates eerie shapes on the wall.
I watch the flames
        never making the same shape twice.

I try to think of better times
when we would talk long into the night.
They're so long ago,
        but I've done so little since then
that the memory is still clear.

The clock on the wall strikes 3 a.m.
and as I slip off,
        attempting to sleep,
I think of how things were …
            when you were here.

# DO YOU STILL LOVE ME?

The long hours,
ticking away one by one,
      are filled with thoughts
          of us together.
Having fun,
walking the streets of the City
in the fog,
   talking about this,
   laughing about that ...
         but everything together.

My thoughts drift to us today ...
   apart ...
         alone.
I'm not sure what happened,
     all I know is you're not here.

The long hours,
     ticking away
         slower than before.
My arms reaching out,
   but you're not here.

Where are you?
Why did you leave?
Will I ever see you again?

Do you still love me?

## CAUTION: ONE WAY

The hollowness of an empty car
        on the drive to Jenner.
The loneliness of the sea
        crashing on an empty beach.
The stillness of a one-way conversation.
A quiet depression sets in on me
       as the sun disappears beyond the horizon.

## SOMEHOW

Somehow it just felt right,
      holding your hand
as we walked among the pines
under the full moon.
I know we had just met,
but I wanted to know
      if you'd hold my hand, too.
And you did.
And more.

Somehow it just felt right
slowly running my fingers through your hair
      and kissing your soft lips.
They were inviting me to, you know.
I just couldn't resist.

Somehow it just felt right
giving you my heart
      as I fell deeply in love with you.
You made it so easy.

Somehow it just felt right,
standing beside you at the altar
    exchanging vows, rings, and I love yous.
Forever lay ahead of us …
      together.

*Jace Carlton*

Somehow it just felt right.

But somehow I didn't see
that it would end like this.
How could I?
I was too much in love with you.

Now my days are empty
because I no longer have you to love ...
    at least not in my arms.

Our friends say I'll be okay,
    given time.
Somehow I know they're right,
but ...
    I can't feel that way yet ...
        not for a long time.

Because I still have your love
to hold in my heart,
I know I'll survive ...

        somehow.

# I'M ONLY ME  ★

When you look at me
take off your rose-colored glasses,
take away any visionary diversion
that might make me larger than life.
I'm only me.
Nothing more.

I won't let myself be designed
          or molded
                    or created by others.
Not by you
     or anyone.

I don't like running races
     with the likes of Clark Kent
          to impress some imaginary Lois Lane.
I just want to be me.

Accept me for that
               or forget it.

# Longing

The seed of love,
once planted and nurtured
with constant love and care,
will never die.

*Jace Carlton*

*Breaking the Stillness*

**WHEN WE'RE AWAY FROM THAT** someone special that we love there's an aching in our heart that can't be satisfied until we're back together again. Seconds feel like hours, hours feel like days, days feel like eternities!

When a relationship ends our hearts may still long for that someone, and in our thoughts and dreams we wish for things to go back to the way they were, or to at least have a chance to try again.

And, when there are missed opportunities, never to come again, we wonder, and may even cry, about the "what ifs" and "if onlys".

These are all a test to see just how strong our hearts are.

## SOMEONE SPECIAL

The darkness of night falls heavy
when you're alone.
The stars come out,
      but they're cold.
They don't sparkle,
they just stare down
      with an emptiness that depresses me.

If you could be here
      I wouldn't be like this.
If I could just hold your hand
      and feel you by my side
it would make all the difference.
Whether you realize it or not,
you do so much to brighten my day
    and shed a light of hope
      in my dark and lonely nights.

I need you near me.

## UXR 324 ★

Your smile was so pretty
    as you stood there.
Dark hair, soft skin, gentle eyes.
And later,
sitting with your two friends,
my eyes were fixed on only you.
You sat quietly, shy ...
with lips that if speaking of love
    would do so with softness.

I wanted to meet you,
but meeting someone in a crowd
is awkward for me.
And even though your crowd
consisted of two friends
I ran scared in the other direction,
    afraid of my feelings for you,
never again to have the chance
of sharing my feelings with you.

And now,
    as you drive off into the night,
I stand alone ...
        not even knowing your name.

## 9:14 ILLINOIS CENTRAL

Midwest plains and little towns
passed along the way,
groves of trees and marble orchards.
Strange names of towns
        like Onarga and Hazel Crest.
The steam passes by the windows
as we make a stop in Kankakee
and little boys stand alone on the platform
waving to the porters,
perhaps wishing they could take a free ride.

It's cold and gray outside
as the 9:14 Illinois Central makes its way to Chicago.
Cold enough for snow and icy ponds
and for children to try out the new ice skates
        they got for Christmas.

But I'd much rather feel the warmth
of you and the California sun,
for that would mean I'd be home
        where I belong.

*Jace Carlton*

# BEACH, 4 A.M.

I walked along the beach,
        it seemed like miles,
    counting all the seagulls
      skirting above the tops of the waves.
Watching the sun set,
        mesmerized by the colors,
    I was wishing you were here with me.

Night came ...
                and loneliness set in.
My arms ached
        longing for you.
I cried out your name ...
I reached out my hand ...
I closed my eyes ...
                and there you were.

## BEACH, 6 P.M.

I spent the day collecting sea shells
    and pieces of driftwood
that I would someday give to you
    as a gift from the sea.
I found a place along the seawall
    and laid down
  just watching the clouds pass
and the seagulls gliding above so effortlessly.
I wished for your hand in mine.

# Hopeful

Listen to your heart,
it will never mislead you …
for only truth is spoken there.

*Jace Carlton*

**WE HOLD OUR BREATH, WE** cross our fingers, we wish upon stars, we even pray.

"Could she be the one?!"

"I've looked for him forever! Oh, I hope everything works out!"

Even those first awkwardly spoken words between two potential lovers are filled with anticipation of what might come to be!

Time stands still! Our hearts pound so loudly we just know everyone can hear it!

We close our eyes. We make a wish. We reach out to hold another's hand.

And we pray they'll never let go.

## HELLO ... ★

I saw you from a distance
and watched you for hours ...
    you didn't even know I was there.

I watched every move you made ...
    the way you smiled and laughed,
        the expression in your eyes
every time you spoke.

I wanted to reach out to you
        hoping you'd notice me
and perhaps
share some of that charm with me.
But I remained silent
    in my thoughts for you ...
wishing I had the courage
            to break the ice.

## SANCTUARY ★

The countless hours I've spent alone ...
        thinking of you.
Footprints I've left on the beach
serve as reminders
        of those lonely days.
Walking slowly,
letting the surf rush over my feet.
        Slowly ...
                slowly.

Slowly passes the time when I'm alone,
but it goes so fast
        when I'm with you.
Slowly,
        like a wave making its way
                toward the shore,
yet it rushes so fast
to go back to the sea.

*Breaking the Stillness*

Now ...
walking through green fields
surrounded by
tree covered hills,
      a quiet sanctuary
where I can retreat
with my thoughts of you.

Thoughts of how much I want you,
how much I need you ...
      and how much I love you.

*Jace Carlton*

## Angel in the Dark

The rain begins to fall
and all around me I feel the walls
      start to close in on me.
It's the start
   of another lonely night
      without you.

Please don't stay away too long …
      the emptiness is unbearable.
You never knew
how your warm embrace delivered me
   from the hungry vulture's glare.
You saved me in time
     to salvage what little life
        I had left in me.
With the kindness
    and patience of an angel
you've brought me back.

How can I ever repay you?

## CLINGING TO LOVE ★

Like the ghostly fog that clings to
hills and marshes,
I cling to every word that
flows over your lips
and every word sounds like love.

*Jace Carlton*

# November

Winter is coming soon
but the last traces of autumn
      still linger.
I love being with you
sharing our lives and our love.
And the only thing good that happens
      when we must part
is that your kiss lingers on my lips
    and in my mind
        until the next time we meet.

## DECEMBER

The evening sun sets and night approaches
finding us in each other's arms.
We kiss ...
and tell each other I love you ...
      yet, we never say a word.

*Jace Carlton*

# THE DAY SPRING CAME

The middle of winter ...
        the midnight air was crisp.
A full moon cast its love over the earth.
Even though we were in a crowd,
we knew nothing of them
since we were lost in a world
        of our own.

"I love you."
For the first time
I heard those words from your lips.
My heart leapt
        and I caught my breath.

A cold night in the middle of winter ...
and yet ...
it was the first day of spring for me.
For someone once said,
"The first day of spring
is the day someone says
        'I love you' ...
                and means it."

*Breaking the Stillness*

# TIMBERLINE ★

Down
      down
            down
the mountain I glided,
not without a million falls.
I saw you down ahead of me
and I was trying so hard
to catch up to you.

I'd watch you ...
    ah-h-h-h,
        what beautiful form.
I was beginning to ask myself
what the heck I was doing skiing ...
    I felt so clumsy compared to you.

One time I saw you
    going up on the chair lift.
I had just taken another spill
when I saw you hop on the chair ...
    I just sat there and stared.
You saw me sprawled out in the snow.
You noticed I was watching you ...
      you smiled ...
           and waved.
I was embarrassed
and got myself up and down the mountain.

*Jace Carlton*

Then I didn't see you
for the longest time.
I had lost you,
    and once again ...
        I felt alone.

I kept going
    down the mountain
    and down on my back,
        time after time,
until I had forgotten
how long I'd been there ...
    without you.

Another spill ...
    I picked myself up.
The trees flew by and then ...
    another spill.
This time I decided
I'd just lie there for a while.

The snow sprayed on me from behind
    as someone made a stop.
I looked up to see who pulled that stunt
        and it was you!
You smiled ...
helped me up ...
    and my fantasy came to life.

## SPRING

Remember the day
    we drove down Lombard Street,
and I stopped near the bottom
and picked some flowers for you
        from someone's garden?

I remember the look on your face
        when I gave them to you.

"Something special for someone special"
is all I said ...
            or needed to say.

## SOFTLY ★

Autumn leaves,
      rustled from the branches by the breeze,
         drifted to the ground,
   as shadows from the late afternoon sun
         danced around you.

You looked my way.
Did you see me?
I wasn't hiding, you know,
    just keeping my distance.
       Wondering.

I turned a page,
attempting to read,
but it was no use.
I looked up but you were gone.
Did the breeze blow you away,
or were you somewhere in the shadows,
playing games?

*Breaking the Stillness*

I turned another page
and the breeze lifted my eyes.
Softly you walked by ...
           and smiled.

Your perfume lingers now.
I'll carry it home with me
     and remember today ...
          and dream of tomorrow.

*Jace Carlton*

## TIME PIECE

You put your memories in boxes
so on a rainy day
you can go through them
and relive the past.

Ticket stubs from movies you cried at.
Corsages from dances you fell in love at.
Sand from your shoes from the first time
we went to Carmel.
A flower from the dozen yellow roses
I gave you on the first day of spring.
A red rose from the dozen roses I gave you
      the night you said "YES!"

What about me?
I have my share of ticket stubs and sand.
They've been safely placed in a box,
      a material time piece,
where the rest of my memories live.

Except those
of your soft lips kissing mine,
or your tender arms
      holding me in an embrace.
Those I keep ...
          only in my heart.

## SURF AND STARS

The surf crashed against the rocks on the shore
and we got soaked
      by the salty spray
we thought we were high enough to miss.
Running up and down the beach all day
had made us hot and sweaty,
and that surf spray felt good
as it cooled us off.

Night will be coming soon
and we'll make a fire to keep us warm.
Later we can roast some marshmallows
and get the sticky mess all over our faces.

As night falls
the stars flood the sky.
The moon hasn't come over the horizon yet.

Were you serious when you asked me
to teach you the constellations?
Or did you just want to get me
out on the beach ...
      all alone ...
           all to yourself?

## LOVE, I

I remember when I used to walk along the beach
      alone.
I'd walk for hours through the surf,
      wondering what it would be like
to share it all with someone.
Sometimes I'd get soaked while sitting on a rock
        too close to the breaking waves,
but never did I lose sight of the day
      when I would share this world with you.

## LOVE, 2 ★

Love doesn't hit everybody
at the same rate of speed.
So I'll slow down
    and wait for you.

Time will pass,
though I know not
      how long,
but I'll continue
    to love you.

## LOVE, 3

A rainy night, a warm fire,
soft music, and you.

That's what love is all about for me.
You, in all your beauty,
surrounding me with all your love.
And me, sitting here,
trying to figure out the reason why
I'm so lucky
        to be the one you love.

# JULIET ★

Ah, Fair Maiden, walking softly ...
    swiftly blows the wind through your hair.
To look upon thee and contemplate my fate
        in this wondrous time called Life!
I pray thee,
    walk past me again,
        and enrich my soul with your beauty!

I cannot hold within,
        longer than this moment,
the memory of you
          without refreshment!

I pray thee come,
      fill my heart with joy!
Smile ...
    then a soft kiss ...
        that may linger on my lips
            and in my memory ...
                forever!

Then,
    if you must ...
        farewell!
            Adieu ...
                Fair Maiden!

*Jace Carlton*

*For Mike & Kay Robertson*

# Two Hearts Are One

Two hearts joining hands,
the fingers of their souls
    intertwine this moment.
An embracing of love
    and a new life,
        together.
Each day they live
will be a brand new day to share.
Smile ... and each day will be happy.
Love ... and each day will be warm.

Yesterday two hearts beat separately,
    each going their own way.
Tomorrow is but a step away from today,
    and yet it's an eternity
        for love to grow in.

*Breaking the Stillness*

Today ...
this moment ...
this man and woman ...
this new life ...
this eternal love ...
and all the caring, sharing,
      and understanding
which is theirs alone.

For Mike and Kay
this is the beginning
of a very beautiful future.

May it begin with a gentle ...
      kiss.

## COMING TOGETHER ... AGAIN

You looked at me softly
with those big brown eyes
and I began to feel
that everything was going to be all right.

It's been a long time
since we were together.
Maybe being apart did us both good.
I think the best thing for us now
is to just take things slowly ...
        one step at a time.

Your quiet mood made you soft and gentle that day.
You filled me with warmth that was boundless.
I saw a different you ...
        and it was beautiful.

## MISTY CLOUDS

I walk along the beach alone.
There's no one else around …
           it's night time.
Mesmerized by the sound of the crashing surf
      my thoughts begin to drift.
Thoughts of you cross my mind
      while the misty clouds pass by the full moon.
The sparkling reflection of the moonlight on the waves
      reminds me of your eyes,
and as each wave rushes to the shore
I think of us and of each time we meet.
The crashing of the waves on the beach
       brings back the feeling of your arms around me
       and you kissing me warmly and tenderly.

But then the waves go back to the sea,
       only to return again,
like you leaving and saying goodbye,
      only to come back again …
           and rush into my arms.

*Jace Carlton*

## DREAMS

You sleep so quietly beside me.
Far off in your world of dreams,
      breathing softly,
           you look so peaceful.
I bend over you
and place a kiss softly on your cheek.
You stir, roll over,
      get comfortable,
    and once again you're off on a cloud.
I watch you for hours
before I finally drift off myself.
I wonder if we'll meet in a dream?

Dream softly, my love.
I'm coming.

# SOMETHING HAPPENED TO ME ON THE WAY TO THE MOON

I was drifting in my thoughts
of running along the beach at midnight,
skydiving in my bright orange flight suit,
driving the Monte Carlo Grand Prix circuit,
and flying to the moon.

Then you came along
and I was no longer drifting,
or seeking the fortunes of the wild.
You've tamed me down,
and once again my feet are firmly planted
      on the ground.

Now there's only one time
when my head is in the clouds …
      when I think of you.

*Jace Carlton*

## SILHOUETTE ★

Notes from my guitar rose in the air
and the London mist
    carried them across her balcony.
Her silhouette emerged through the curtain
    and, with a gentle nod,
encouraged me to play on.
Looking back to the city lights
my balcony concert continued …
      with an audience of one.
An hour passed, perhaps more,
before retreating to my room,
    her silhouette now a memory.
Was she ever really there?

On my balcony before dawn,
I waited to see if she would rise
    before the sun.
I wanted …
      I needed to see her eyes and her smile.
Was it too early,
    or … was I too late?
My guitar waited just inside my room.
No … not this early.

Somehow … I knew she was gone.
I asked around, but …
      how do you describe a silhouette?
I lost her in the crowd of days.

*Breaking the Stillness*

Coach rides through the countryside,
a ferry across the channel,
more nights in different cities,
    playing for strangers.
Weeks passed.
Her silhouette now a beautiful,
  but haunting memory.

A full moon rose
    over the courtyard of the ancient castle,
as notes from my guitar
were carried by the summer breeze
      toward the river below.
I was playing for the lovers.

You smiled at me from across the way,
and when my music was over
    you invited me to walk with you in the moonlight.

We found a soft place to lie on the grass
down near the river,
and there you told me
how this evening reminded you …
    of one night in London,
      not that long ago …
when you softly fell asleep …
        to my balcony concert.

# Songs

To love a person
is to learn the song that is in their heart
and sing it to them
when they have forgotten.

*Arne Garborg*

**MUSIC CAN STIR OUR SOULS,** but words can touch our hearts and lift us higher than we can ever imagine because they tell *our* stories!

We talk in words, we sing in words, and the written word comes alive, stirring our imaginations!

I have a few very special songs that have meant everything to me for what seems like an eternity. I've heard it said that all it takes is one song to release a million memories and, at least in my case, that's absolutely true!

I can hear a particular song and it will take me back to a very special time in my life when I was on top of the world in love! More than once one or two particular songs have lifted and sustained me when I felt I'd lost everything.

What songs have meant the most to you throughout your life? Were they upbeat, making you want to jump up and dance? Or were they soft and mellow, making you want to hold that someone special and dance *really* slow and never let them go?

Whichever it is (or, perhaps, somewhere in between) nearly everyone's heart and soul are stirred by songs. They are the lifeblood that connects us all.

I share with you a few that I've written during times of love, as well as times of loss.

Searching … always searching … for the perfect way to say …

"I love you", "I miss you", "I need you", or "I'm sorry".

# LOVIN' YOU

Wonder where I've been?
Well, I've been lookin' around, too.
Beating back more memories,
cuz I've never stopped lovin' you.

Lookin' back to that night
holdin' each other so close,
never knowing that tomorrow
would become a haunting ghost.

> I've been tryin' to be strong in all the broken places,
> tryin' to avoid memories that my heart chases.
> Somewhere between the hidden
>     and the almost full moon
> you can always find me lovin' you.
> Yeah, you can always find me lovin' you.

Holdin' on to hope against hope
you're always on my mind,
while I'm on this journey
among the lost and left behind.

> I've been tryin' to be strong in all the broken places
> tryin' to avoid memories that my heart chases.
> Somewhere between the hidden
>     and the almost full moon
> you can always find me lovin' you.
> Yeah, you can always find me lovin' you.

*Jace Carlton*

Once there was a love so rare,
like no one else would ever know.
Now the pain leaves a heart bare,
like a willow in the snow.

I've been tryin' to be strong in all the broken places
tryin' to avoid memories that my heart chases.
Somewhere between the hidden
    and the almost full moon
you can always find me lovin' you.

Yeah, somewhere between the hidden
    and the almost full moon
you can always find me …
                  lovin' you.

# No One to Remember Your Name

Walkin' down familiar streets,
past homes and schools I used to know.
Memories of playing catch
or building castles in the snow.

Drove by the house where I used to live
all those years ago.
Took a photo, but it's not the same.
Where'd all my friends go?

> Well, they say you can't go home again,
> that things just aren't the same.
> There's no one there that was there back then,
> and no one to remember your name.

Whatever we did way back then
is only in our memory.
So even if you go home again,
you'll be lonely just like me.

*Jace Carlton*

Yeah, they say you can't go home again,
that things just aren't the same.
There's no one there that was there back then,
and no one to remember your name.

    If I could only turn back time
    to the way things were back then.
    Baseball in the spring and football in the fall,
    what I wouldn't give to go home again.

Yeah, they say you can't go home again,
that things just aren't the same.
There's no one there now that was there back then …
there's no one to remember your name.

# IN MY MEMORY

Searching through an old cardboard box
for a special memory,
a photograph of your angel face
that you framed and gave to me.
I remember the way you looked at me
and then I heard you say

> Baby, I'll be yours forever,
> forever and a day.
> We will always be together
> and I will always stay
> right by your side, and inside your heart
> is where I always want to be.
> That's what you said way back then
> in my memory.

I came across a seashell
from that special night.
A moonlight walk along the beach
and when I held you tight
you looked at me with those emerald eyes.
I can still hear you say

*Jace Carlton*

Baby, I'll be yours forever,
forever and a day.
We will always be together
and I will always stay
right by your side, and inside your heart
is where I always want to be.
That's what you said way back then
in my memory.

> That fateful night I lost you
> and God took you away.
> What would I give, what would I do
> for one more time to hear you say

Baby, I'll be yours forever,
forever and a day
we will always be together
and I will always stay
right by your side, and inside your heart
is where I always want to be.
That's what you said way back then
in my memory.

I feel you deep inside my heart
and that's where you'll always be.
I'll keep our love safe and warm
in my memory.

*Breaking the Stillness*

*For Janet and Foster Mullen*

# THE ONE ★

He comes along
he steals your heart
he takes your hand
the loving starts.

The sun comes up
the moon does, too.
The stars shine bright
for just you two.

>You make a wish upon a star
>that you can stay the way you are.
>He kisses you, you feel it too,
>that he's the one.

Each day goes by
just like the past.
You know this love
will always last.

It feels so good
you feel so blessed,
you say a prayer
held to your breast.

*Jace Carlton*

       And when you look into his eyes
       it's then that you both realize
       he has your heart, you have his, too.
       Yes, he's the one.

Growing closer
day by day,
loving stronger
in every way.

And then one night
he's gone from you.
You can't go on.
What will you do?

       Across all time and space
       the love you share can't be erased.
       You reach for him, he knows you do,
       he'll always be the one for you.
       God's loving grace will hold you two.
       Yes, he's ... the one.

# IF WE EVER LOVE AGAIN ★

We used to be so in love
we were always together,
hand in hand, day by day,
we just knew it would last forever.

But then one day the devil came
and broke us apart.
Now I'm left with shattered dreams
and an aching in my heart.

> If we ever love again
> I'll be sure to let you know
> that I'll love you to the end
> and never let you go.
> If we ever, if we ever love again.

I've tried to find you everywhere,
but the only place I see you
is in my dreams late at night,
but I can never reach you.

*Jace Carlton*

I'll keep searching every day
I never will give up
till I'm holding you in my arms
and giving you all my love.

    If we ever love again
    I'll be sure to let you know
    that I'll love you to the end
    and never let you go.
    If we ever, if we ever love again.

        Across all time and space
        are you searching for me, too?
        Sometimes I wonder,
        and I really wish I knew.

If we ever love again
I'll be sure to let you know
that I'll love you to the end
and never let you go.
If we ever ...
    if we ever love again.

# ETERNALLY ★

I've searched all over
for a true love
someone who'd always stay.
Someone to hold
and love me tender
and chase my blues away.

And then it happened
out of nowhere …
it took me by surprise.
When I saw you
my heart just melted
my dreams were in your eyes.

Give me all your love, oh darling,
your heart is safe with me.
Give me kisses ever-flowing
I'll give my love
eternally.

*Jace Carlton*

Come to me, darling.
Take that first step
to make my dreams all come true.
I'll make you mine
and then together
we'll make the stars shine through.

This perfect moment
whisper softly
that you will always be true.
All I need is
your love forever.
My love
is for you, Love,
just you.

# CROSSROADS

We've traveled down some rough roads
almost lost our way a time or two,
but we've made it through together
and it should be clear to you
that our love is getting stronger
with every passing day
but you seem to doubt me.
What more can I say?

> Baby, we're at the crossroads
> and I know which way to go.
> Just take my hand and trust in me
> and then, you too, will know.
> Our hearts will beat as one
> as we take this step together.
> Just take my hand and trust in me.
> and I'll take you to forever.

*Jace Carlton*

You've been searching for that one word
that would make it all so clear.
How we feel about each other
the word you need to hear.
But love's a strange thing, babe,
and one word won't make it true.
It's your heart that's going to let you know
how much that I love you.

      Baby, we're at the crossroads
      and I know which way to go.
      Just take my hand and trust in me
      and then, you too, will know.
      Our hearts will beat as one
      as we take this step together.
      Just take my hand and trust in me.
      and I'll take you to forever.

      Just take my hand and trust in me
      and I'll love you ... forever.

# THE EDGE OF FOREVER
# AND GOODBYE ★

Once we had the time
to walk hand in hand,
to run through the ocean waves
and lie upon the sand.

Once we had the time
to kiss like lovers,
and cry at old movies,
and laugh with each other.

> Livin' on the edge
> of forever and goodbye,
> not knowing whether
> I'm gonna live or die.
> Wonderin' if you ever loved me,
> or has it been a lie?
> You've got me livin' on the edge
> of forever and goodbye.

*Jace Carlton*

Once we had the need
to see each other through.
Ah-h-h, the toughest of times,
they were so few.

Once we had it all,
but I guess you wanted more.
How could I have known
what you had in store?

> Livin' on the edge
> of forever and goodbye,
> not knowing whether
> I'm gonna live or die.
> Wonderin' if you ever loved me,
> or has it been a lie?
> You've got me livin' on the edge
> of forever and goodbye.

*Breaking the Stillness*

>Maybe if things were different,
>maybe if times were hard,
>maybe we'd have pulled each other closer
>from the very start.

Livin' on the edge
of forever and goodbye,
not knowing whether
I'm gonna live or die.
Wonderin' if you ever loved me,
or has it been a lie?
You've got me livin' on the edge
of forever and goodbye.

Wonderin' if you ever loved me,
or has it been a lie?
You've got me livin' on the edge
of forever and goodbye.

Goodbye.

*Jace Carlton*

# A PLACE FOR HER PIANO ★

You're looking for a place
where the lights are low,
the music's sweet,
and the drinks poured slow.

I know just the place,
called Indigo Blue,
and there's a singer there
to mend a heart or two.

>Let her sing her music.
>Let her touch your heart.
>She will work her magic
>when it's broken all apart.
>All she needs is a little time,
>she likes to take it slow.
>So make way for the lady
>and a place for her piano.

*Breaking the Stillness*

She sings her way
through a melody or two,
and then one song
has its way with you.

Your heart beats faster
and you know it's true.
She's singing a song
meant only for you.

>Let her sing her music.
>Let her touch your heart.
>She will work her magic
>when it's broken all apart.
>All she needs is a little time,
>she likes to take it slow.
>So make way for the lady
>and a place for her piano.

*Jace Carlton*

She can take you places you never knew before.
She can pick your heart up and make it soar.
And just when you think you can't take anymore
she'll set you down easy
    and you'll be begging for more.
Yes, she can take you places you never knew before,
then she'll leave you with a feeling
    you just can't ignore.

    Let her sing her music.
    Let her touch your heart.
    She will work her magic
    when it's broken all apart.
    All she needs is a little time
    as the candles glow.
    So make way for the lady
    and a place for her piano.

    All she needs is a little time
    as the candles glow.
    So make way for the lady …

and a place for her piano.

# Another Lonely New Year's Eve ★

The house is quiet as I sit by the fire
looking back on the year about to expire
hoping the new year will bring something new
as my thoughts drift back to you.

It's been too long since I looked in your eyes
and felt your love and heard our sighs.
It's been too long since I was in your arms,
back when you were mine.

> The crowd in Times Square is going wild
> and the ball is coming down.
> Another year is passing by
> as confetti hits the ground.
> Some look forward to what's yet to come,
> but it's just another year to me,
> as I drink a toast with no one
> on another lonely New Year's Eve.

*Jace Carlton*

The calendar's turned, another year's gone by,
I'll try to keep busy, I don't want to cry.
But it's no use, I can't play this part,
you haunt every place in my lonely heart.

Now the fire is embers as I rise from my chair,
stumble through the darkness and climb the stairs.
Sleep will avoid me for hours on end
'til I finally drift off to dream of you again.

> The crowd in Times Square is going wild
> and the ball is coming down.
> Another year is passing by
> as confetti hits the ground.
> Some look forward to what's yet to come,
> but it's just another year to me,
> as I drink a toast with no one
> on another lonely New Year's Eve.

*Breaking the Stillness*

Sometimes I wonder if I'll ever love again,
and all I can do is pray.
Or wish and hope and wonder
if you'll come back home to stay.

The crowd in Times Square is going wild
and the ball is coming down.
Another year is passing by
as confetti hits the ground.
Some look forward to what's yet to come,
but it's just another year to me,
as I drink a toast with no one
on another lonely New Year's Eve.

As I drink a toast with no one
on another lonely New Year's Eve.

# RIGHT HERE WAITING *
(A DUET)

(Male)
I know sometimes I seem distant,
I really don't mean to be.
I guess there's something on my mind
that's been tormenting me.
You held me in your arms tonight
and tenderly you asked me,

> (Female) (Chorus)
> Why can't you love me
> the way that I love you?
> And do you ever think of me
> the way I think of you?
> And will you hold me in your dreams tonight
> just the way I hold you in my arms so tight?
> I hope someday you'll find the way
> 'til then I want you to know
> I'm right here waiting,
> I'm right here waiting.

(Male)
There's something keeping me from loving you
no matter how hard I try.
I wish that I could let it go
so I wouldn't see you cry.
You wiped the tears from those emerald eyes
and tenderly asked me one more time

> (Female) (Chorus)
> Why can't you love me
> the way that I love you?
> And do you ever think of me
> the way I think of you?
> And will you hold me in your dreams tonight,
> just the way I hold you in my arms so tight?
> I hope someday you'll find the way
> 'til then I want you to know
> I'm right here waiting,
> I'm right here waiting.

(Male)
I've struggled for so very long
to find out what's going on,
and I realized I never let her go …
yeah, my heart never let her go.

*Jace Carlton*

(Male) (spoken, almost whispered)
Cuz my heart cries
Why can't she love me
the way I still love her?
And does she ever think of me
the way I still think of her?
And why can't I hold her in my arms tonight
the way I used to hold her, oh so tight?

One of these nights
    through all my tears maybe I'll realize
        it's over
        (female echo) > and I'll be waiting
        it's over
        (female echo) > and I'll be waiting
        it's ... over   (slowly and very softly)
        it's over. (softly spoken)
        (female)  I'm right here waiting.

# Behind the Muse

# My Muse, the Stories, and Other Things

**I HAVE LOST TRACK OF** the number of times in my life that I have been asked if I have a Muse that inspires me to write and my answer is yes, and no.

Yes, because I believe it's a romantic concept to think of a Muse whispering thoughts and ideas into my mind regarding what to write about. Yes, because of how she can help me phrase a particular emotion or feeling, or how to paint a scene in just the perfect way for the reader to feel like they are right there in that scene and feeling the very emotions my characters are going through. Truth be told, I quite often feel them myself as I'm writing.

No, because I know exactly where those thoughts and ideas come from … my Heavenly Father. He is the one who has blessed me with the ability to express myself through writing and speaking since I was in elementary school. It has just been up to me to put the effort into making it all happen. And when I do … well, let's just say that is when the magic begins.

I like to think that I have been blessed with the best of both worlds - two awesome shoulder angels, my Muse whispering to me in one ear, and the Holy Spirit whispering in the other, both helping me to give my very best.

The ideas can start from nearly anything I see or hear, even a scent can trigger a distant memory and bring it back into full remembrance, and it will not be long before the words begin to flow. I am often asked at book signings about these moments, and I have enjoyed sharing those more intimate moments with those in attendance and hope you will find at least one of your favorites in this collection of thoughts. If not, I invite you to write to me through the publisher's address on the copyright page. I promise to respond to every letter I receive.

I must confess that many of the poems I wrote in my early years were strictly from my imagination; one example of this is *Beach, 4 a.m.* It was not until over two years after I had written that poem that I was actually at the beach at 4 a.m. But, I *had* been at the beach late on many nights (usually leaving around midnight), and I had stayed up all night many times at youth conventions as well as studying for finals, so I simply combined those experiences with what I had actually seen late at night at the beach, let my imagination run for how much more quiet it would be at 4 a.m., and put pen to paper!

On the other side of the coin, many of my poems and lyrics were based on real life experiences, either mine or one of my friends, and there are many examples of that throughout this book, including *Hello…* and *Another Lonely New Year's Eve*.

I have also been inspired by photographs that I have seen, whether framed in gift shops, on greeting cards or posters, or even on the covers of books or magazines. I let my imagination run wild and let those photographs tell a story that no one else might otherwise see. *Please Write, Clinging to Love, November, December, Sanctuary*, and *Juliet* are such examples.

Whatever the source of inspiration might be for me I am truly grateful I am able to share these poems, lyrics, and stories with you. If these poems and songs make you smile, laugh, cry, or want to dance (or any combination of those), then you and I will have connected across time and distance.

Oh, by the way ... the name of my Muse is Kiera.

Now, let's get started, shall we?!

## CHRISTMAS, 1969 (p. 10)

**WHILE SIMPLE IN ITS FORM,** those two words said everything about my state of mind at that time. I had been with a wonderful young lady for over two years when things began to go wrong. We tried hard to make things work, but I guess things just got too hard for her, and at the end of November she decided that it was over. The devastation I felt over the loss seemed insurmountable. Suicide was *never* an option, but I just had no idea how I could go on without her. Sleepless nights, long days that never seemed to end ... she was everything to me, and now she was gone.

The days stretched into weeks; the weeks into months, and the years ... well, let's just say that it took many years to be able to fully move on.

## TOWEL (p. 11)

**AT ONE POINT WHEN I** was writing so many poems about love I thought to myself, 'I wonder if I could write about something else?' I was just about to shave to get ready for a date when I noticed a towel hanging from a rack near the sink. 'Hmmm,' I thought. 'Okay, a towel it is!' and after I had shaved and before getting dressed for my date I sat down at my desk and let the words just flow. Hmmmmm ... it turned into a poem about love after all! I guess that's just what I get for being a hopeless, card-carrying, incurable romantic!

# PLEASE WRITE (p. 16)

**ABOUT A MONTH OR SO** after I had started dating this one particular young lady, we stopped briefly at my apartment to get something before continuing on our date. She asked if she could come up and see my apartment and I had no problem with that because I always kept it clean and organized.

While I was looking for what we had stopped for, she walked slowly around my apartment, looking at the photographs on the walls and the poems next to them.

"Did you write all of these?" she asked in astonishment.

"Yes," I replied casually, but inwardly I was excited because *she* was so excited.

"I didn't know you wrote poetry. These are good!"

"Thank you." I started to feel my face turn red from embarrassment at her enthusiasm.

"So, did you find the photo first and then write about it, or did you write the poem and then just happen to find a photo later that would tie in with it?"

"The photo came first."

She went back to looking at the other photos and reading the accompanying poems. A few minutes later I found what I had been looking for and we left.

As we were driving to San Francisco for our date I noticed that this normally talkative young lady was rather quiet and I asked her if everything was all right.

"Yes!" she answered excitedly. It was pretty obvious that I had interrupted her train of thought. "Sorry, I was just thinking."

"About?"

"How long have you been writing?"

"Poems? I started when I was thirteen, and I started writing lyrics about six months later."

"You write songs, too?!?!"

"Yes, but mostly just the lyrics."

"Wow! Have you published any of your poems or recorded any of your songs?"

"No."

"No, you haven't published any of your poems, or no, you haven't recorded any of your songs?"

"Both."

"Why *not!!*"

"I don't know. I just write for myself mostly."

"Why?"

"Because … they're very personal, and what I write is just okay. I don't think they're good enough to be published."

"Are you kidding me?! From what I just read up in your apartment they are great!"

I just smiled and thanked her as I continued to drive.

"Seriously, you need to get those poems published!"

"Someday … maybe."

She sat back and sighed, and we rode on quietly for another few minutes before she looked at me.

"May I ask you a favor?"

"Sure, I guess so."

"I have a greeting card at home with a nice photograph on the front. Do you think you could write a poem about it for me?"

"I'd have to see the card first before I could say yes."

"Okay. I'll bring it with me on our next date."

"Sounds good," and off we went to the City with nothing more being mentioned about my writing for the rest of the evening.

The next weekend we were heading to the City again and on the drive she reached for her purse and pulled out a greeting card.

"This is the card I was telling you about last weekend. Do you think you could write something to that photo?"

I took one look at it. "Yes! Absolutely!" She smiled, handed me the card, and I put it above my visor. After our date that night I took it in, looked at it for a while, then set it on my desk. I turned on my stereo, grabbed my headphones, and sat down on the sofa to relax before heading to bed.

Lying in bed I had that photo in my mind. It was a soft focus photo of a young lady in a long print dress sitting at a writing table with a pen in her hand. She was looking off in the distance as if she were thinking about what she wanted to write.

The next afternoon I looked at the card again and some ideas started to flow, but evenings have always been my best writing time, so I set it aside again. Later that evening I put some mood music on the stereo, sat down at my desk, looked at the card again, and everything came together!

## I'M ONLY ME (p. 25)

**NEARLY ALL OF THE POEMS** and lyrics I've written throughout my life have been about love, either the joy of finding and sharing love, or the pain of loss and searching for answers that go forever unanswered. *I'm Only Me* was different.

Oh, it *did* have to do with someone I was in love with, but it was a difficult break up. We'd known each other as friends for quite a while, but we'd only been dating for a couple of months when I felt something just wasn't right. My feelings were answered a short time later when she called me one evening and asked if she could come over. The tone in her voice wasn't excited as it had always been before, but more reserved, more ... serious.

She arrived at my apartment about fifteen minutes later and we sat and talked for only a short time before it was clear we were over. She took a deep breath, reached for her purse, got up, and left.

I was falsely accused of trying to be someone I wasn't, when, ever since we'd met I'd just been myself, nothing more.

I didn't know how to be anything or anyone else. The fault, apparently, was in her mind and her expectations of me. Mad and frustrated, I sat in the living room for an hour or so with the lights off. Then, still mad and frustrated, I got up and walked to my desk, and out flowed *I'm Only Me*.

# UXR 324 (p. 32)

**MY BEST FRIEND, MIKE, WAS** given three free passes to see Henry Mancini in concert in San Francisco; the only catch was that we had to be ushers until about 15-20 minutes after the concert started and then we were allowed to sit anywhere we wanted. So he and I and our mutual friend, Tim, headed for the City for a great evening. We just had no idea how great it would end up being!

The concert, itself, was so much fun! Part way through the evening we were stunned when we noticed our old high school choir director, Tom Hart, perform the saxophone solo for *The Pink Panther Theme*! After the concert we worked our way down to the main level and up to the stage as fast as we could in order to try to catch Mr. Hart before he headed for the dressing rooms. He was just about to head that way when we called out to catch his attention. He turned around and saw us waving so he stepped toward the front of the stage.

We told him how excited we were to see him and asked how he was lucky enough to play with Henry that night. He explained that every time Henry came to the Bay Area he would call and invite him to play, and especially perform the solo on *The Pink Panther Theme*! We chatted for a few more minutes until he said he needed to go, so we said goodbye and headed out into the night.

However, it was a beautiful evening in late July and there was just *no way* we were going to head home that early! We thought about what else we might do in the City and we all agreed on heading to the Ghirardelli Chocolate Manufactory for hot fudge sundaes!

When we arrived we found a comfortable booth. Mike and Tim sat across from me, facing the door. While waiting for our orders to arrive we talked and laughed, recalling many fun times we shared in high school. Our orders arrived and our eyes grew wide! SO much ice cream! So much fudge sauce! And so much whipped cream! We wasted no time at all and dug right in!

In the midst of enjoying our tall, decadent, and overflowing goblets of delight, Tim was about to take another scoop from his goblet when his arm suddenly froze in mid-air and his jaw dropped as his gaze was focused on the entrance to the restaurant. I glanced toward Mike and his gaze was also aimed directly toward the entrance, so I turned and looked over my shoulder at what had caught their complete attention ... three beautiful young ladies had just walked in! A few moments later they were sitting just two tables away! Our hopes for a great evening had just taken a quantum leap!

The three of us very quietly discussed which of these young ladies we were interested in meeting, and fortunately each of us had chosen a different girl. Now the only question was ... what were we going to actually *do* about it?! For some reason, Mike and Tim looked at *me* to make the first move, *whatever* that might be!

While we were discussing our dilemma, the young ladies had placed their orders and we promptly slowed down so we wouldn't finish too far ahead of them. We'd glance over toward their table and notice that they were already looking at us. A few minutes later they'd look over at us and notice we were already looking at them. Back and forth the tango went, but neither Mike, Tim, nor I had the guts to make the first move. It reminded me of dances in junior high when we'd all stand around listening to the great music but no one danced because the guys were too chicken to ask any of the girls to dance! SO many missed opportunities!

Despite our best effort to take our time we were finished and ready to go. Although it was a Wednesday evening and not a Friday or Saturday night, the restaurant was busy because of so many people wanting to enjoy something cool on such a warm evening. We figured we had better leave so someone else could have our booth.

We gradually got up, casually glanced once again toward the young ladies, noticed that they were watching us, then paid our bill and left; but we didn't go far!

As we stepped out into the night we felt a cool breeze from the bay gently blowing through the Square. We decided to wait until the girls left so we found a place off to one side where we could see them as they left and could then follow them for a while to see where they might go next.

Our wait wasn't very long at all. As they came out, they turned right and headed toward the steps that led down to the sidewalk that runs along Ghirardelli Square and toward the bay. We followed at a very comfortable distance so if they noticed us they wouldn't be concerned. They crossed the street, and so did we. 'Where are they going?' I wondered.

About a block and a half down the hill I noticed the young lady that I had had my eye on step back out into the street as they approached a lone parked car. She stopped, opened the door, and then unlocked the door on the other side so her friends could get in.

'Oh, NO! Where are they going?!' We quickly walked closer and I was able to catch the description of the car, a 1968 Mustang Fastback. The engine started, and a moment later they pulled away, drove down the street, turned the corner at the bottom of the hill, and drove off into the night.

Sighhhhhh ....................

While waiting for traffic lights to change I occasionally like to glance at license plates just to see if there are any interesting or unusual ones. Many years ago, while still living in California, and while waiting at a signal near our home, I was behind a 1968 Mustang Fastback and casually glanced at the license plate. I began to read 'UXR' and I held my breath!!!! I continued 3! ....... 2! ......... 5! Sighhhhh ..... oh, SO close! I have *no* idea what I would have done if it had been the car from that wonderful night in San Francisco all those years ago, but for a brief moment I relived that whole evening … and it brought a smile to my face.

# HELLO ... (p. 41)

**I ATTENDED THE WEDDING FOR** my buddy, Jim, whom I had grown up living next door to. During the ceremony I noticed one of the bridesmaids in particular, and later, during the reception, I noticed her standing all alone across the room and wanted to talk with her, but my introverted side kicked in and I hesitated for just a second. Just then two other guys approached her, followed a moment later by a third, and they all talked with her for a long time. Too long. I kept my distance and glanced over toward her from time to time just to see if I might get a chance to talk with her, but she was engaged in talking with more and more people. At one point we made eye contact for more than just a moment, and she smiled, but someone distracted her and that moment vanished.

As the reception was about to end I had the chance to chat with Jim and his beautiful new bride, Nancy. I was able to get her name, but when I turned around to look for her one last time I didn't see her. That night I wrote this poem.

I waited until I knew Jim and Nancy were home from their honeymoon and then called to find out more about her as well as her phone number. I called her, introduced myself, and we chatted for about an hour.

We dated twice and had some fun, found some common interests such as Italian food (especially pizza), playing the guitar, listening to LPs by Carly Simon, Carole King, and Neil Diamond, along with Robert Redford movies. Then her ex-boyfriend unexpectedly came back into the picture. End of story.

## SANCTUARY (p. 42)

*SANCTUARY* **IS ANOTHER POEM THAT** was inspired by a photo. It was actually a gift plaque I found in a Hallmark store.

The poem begins with a young man walking along the beach (which I often loved to do) while thinking of the girl he loved. Then the setting changes to the actual scene in the photo, where he's walking through a wooded park with sunlight streaming through a few of the branches of the trees in the background.

I remember the afternoon I wrote this poem was sunny with a cool breeze blowing through my bedroom windows which enhanced the feeling I got for the wooded park in the photo.

## CLINGING TO LOVE (p. 45)

**I WAS SHOPPING AT OUR** local mall one evening many years ago when I stopped into one of my favorite stores. They sold everything from books, to posters, greeting cards, and gifts, along with everything you might need or want in the way of art supplies.

As I wandered through the cards and posters section I made a wonderful discovery! Hallmark had just come out with a new line of greeting cards that was quite unique. As usual, they offered a variety of messages within the cards themselves along with 21 different photos you could choose from to slip into the front half of the card, depending on your mood and the message in the card.

I looked at the different photos and immediately knew that I could write something for each one. Because I was a regular customer I had become good friends with the manager, Jill, so I selected one of each of the photos and approached her and presented her with a question about the possibility of only buying just one of each of the photos without having to buy a full set of cards to go with them. She smiled and her eyes got really big.

"Really? I've never been asked anything like that before!"

"Well, have you ever had a set of greetings cards quite like this before?" She paused a moment before responding.

"Hmmm, no I guess not. But ... I would have no idea how to price them. Are there any of the regular cards that go with the set that you'd also be interested in buying along with the photos?"

"No, just these photos."

She looked at the photos I had handed her and replied, "I'm afraid I'll have to charge you the full amount for each one."

It didn't take me long to think about it. "Deal!"

She smiled as she stepped behind the counter to ring up the sale. "Do you mind if I ask why you only want the photos?"

"Not at all. I'm a writer, and each of these photos has a story to tell and I intend to tell it."

"Really?! How wonderful!"

"Thanks!"

As she slipped my photos into a paper bag with my receipt she wished me luck and added, "I'd love to read one of them someday."

"Sure!"

I headed home after that and sat down at my desk, spreading out the photos in front of me. There seemed to be a couple of "themes" to the variety. They were all photos of nature settings, and a few had a guy or a girl or a couple in them. There also seemed to be a kind of "seasonal" feel to the whole collection. Ideas began to form of what each photo might "say", but none were strong enough to make me want to start writing right then, so I stacked them up and set them on the corner of my desk. The next morning I popped them into my backpack as I headed out for another day of college classes.

From time to time during the day I'd take them out while I was waiting for another class to begin and ideas were still simmering just below the surface. Then, with a few extra minutes before my last class of the day, everything fell into place and I immediately began to write! I finished the first poem shortly after the professor had begun his lecture. About halfway through the class I was just too distracted to concentrate so I slipped the cards out of my backpack and found another photo that "spoke to me". Before the class was over the second poem was complete and I was on a roll!

After class I headed to my part time job after which I went home, ate a quick dinner, and then it was back to my desk to work on those photos!

Photo after photo, poem after poem, everything just flowed so effortlessly! I'd *never* written so many poems in such a short period of time. Most usually took me anywhere from a few hours to a few days to complete, occasionally longer in order to get it *just right*. Before I wrapped things up and headed to bed I'd written eleven poems!

The next morning I debated about going to my classes or to just stay home and write, but then I remembered a test I needed to take in one of my classes so the decision was made. I put the photos into my backpack and I was off.

I took advantage of spare moments throughout the day and just before my last class that afternoon I had finished my last poem! Twenty one poems in less than twenty four hours! Never before or since have different ideas flowed so easily.

Each of those poems appeared in the manuscript for my second book, *Rainwater Tapestry*, but only four, *Clinging to Love, November, December,* and *Spring* made into *Breaking the Stillness*.

The setting for *Clinging to Love* was a photo of a foggy morning with the fog so thick you could barely see trees in the distance across a meadow.

Post note: A week later I returned to the store, bought just one card from that set, along with just the right photo, then went home and wrote the poem in the card and returned to the store that evening and gave it to Jill. She was thrilled!

Post Note Two: Just before my first book of poetry, *Sounds of Darkness*, was published I shared my excitement with Jill and she replied, "Be sure to let me know when your book is available and I'll order a dozen to sell here in our store!" I enthusiastically thanked her and was on my way. A few months later she made good on that promise, and a couple of weeks after that she called me and ordered more copies because the first order had already sold out! When I dropped off the new order she thanked me and then surprised me again.

"I've been thinking ... I would love to host a book signing party for you. What do you think?"

For a moment I just stood there, stunned, not knowing what to say! Finally I replied, "Sure!!"

She decided to hold it on the Saturday before Valentine's Day and advertised it heavily with posters in the store windows, as well as flyers she printed that went into every shopping bag. Needless to say, it was a great party!

## TIMBERLINE (p. 49)

**I TOOK AN ALL TOO** brief unplanned trip to Oregon one winter because I just wanted (needed?) to get away. I had some friends I thought about visiting, but I was also thinking about making a stop at Timberline Lodge on Mt. Hood in northern Oregon. I had been there only once before when I was on vacation in Oregon and Washington with my parents during the summer I turned eight.

The Lodge was everything I remembered and more, because when I had been there with my parents it was in the summer and everything was dry and hot, but this time it was in the middle of winter, it had snowed a lot, and I had to put chains on my car in order to make it up the mountain.

I was a freelance photographer at the time, and I was hoping to get some great shots of the area. Between the shots I took of the Lodge and the sunset that night, as well as the sunrise the next morning, the trip was definitely a winner.

As I mentioned, this trip was unplanned, and so, unfortunately, were my expenses. I had to be so tight with my budget that I dared not actually spend the night *in* the Lodge, but I did stay *at* the Lodge ... in the parking lot ... in my car ... freezing.

Well, I didn't exactly freeze *all* night long; when it got too cold I started the engine and let the heater warm everything up until I was nice and warm, and then I'd turn it off again to save gas. I was also lucky enough to pick up a popular radio station from San Francisco, 620 miles to the south! I didn't sleep at all that night, but no big deal. I was young and still crazy enough to pull something like that off without a problem.

As the sky began to lighten I wrapped my scarf around my neck, zipped up my coat, ignored my ski gloves (have you ever tried to shoot a Nikon camera with ski gloves on? I didn't think so), grabbed my camera, and headed out to get some more great shots.

Most of my poems and lyrics tell brief 3-4 minute stories, and *Timberline* is one of them. Although I didn't do any skiing while I was there, this story is about a guy who has a chance meeting with a pretty girl on the slopes. The actual story took place in the Lodge.

A few hours after I arrived I was hungry and headed to the restaurant to eat. Although I knew I didn't have enough money in my budget to spend the night, I wasn't going to miss the chance to enjoy a nice meal.

I had my journal with me and was jotting down some notes as I sat alone at my table. After a few minutes I looked up and glanced casually around the warm and comfortable dining room. The restaurant was filling up nicely, even for being the middle of the week.

Off to my right I noticed a young lady a few tables away sitting by herself. Was she waiting for someone? As our eyes met she quickly looked away, but I noticed she was smiling. I looked back down at my journal, and wrote down another brief note or two before glancing her way again. She was already looking at me, but this time she didn't look away. She smiled, I smiled, and we held that glance a few moments longer, and then her waiter came to take her order. I went back to my journal.

Before I knew it that same waiter was asking me if I had had a chance to look at the menu. I said I had and gave him my order. As he left, the stranger at the other table came into view again, and she was looking my way.

'What's going on?' I thought.

After holding our glance for a few moments I looked back down at my journal but didn't write anything, I just sat there wondering. 'What *is* going on? Do I know her from somewhere? High school? College? And we just happen to be at the same place at the same time many years later?' I was too nervous to look her way again so I started to write some more notes in my journal.

Moments later I noticed out of the corner of my eye the waiter had walked up to my table, but not to deliver my dinner. He handed me a note. I looked at him quizzically and he smiled and stepped aside just a bit as he motioned behind him.

"It's from the young lady at the other table." I looked over toward her and she was smiling, shyly. I opened the note. It simply read, "Hi."

I smiled to myself, then toward her, and then wrote, "Hi. I couldn't help but notice that you're by yourself. Are you alone? If so, would you be interested in having some company for dinner?" I handed the note back to our smiling waiter and watched as he delivered it.

As he handed her the note, she thanked him and then glanced at me before opening it. As she read it I noticed her sweet smile growing just a little brighter. She closed the note, then ever so briefly closed her eyes, and then looked at me and nodded. I quickly gathered my things, and as I was walking toward her I asked our waiter to please bring my meal to her table when it was ready. He smiled and replied, "My pleasure, sir."

As I sat down we introduced ourselves and I took a deep breath and said, "Thank you."

"For what?" she asked.

"For smiling, and for saying 'Hi'."

"Well, thank you for offering to join me."

Now that our initial polite comments were over, what next?? I had never done anything like this before so I was nervous about where this would go. She broke the stillness.

"I couldn't help notice that you kept writing something in your notebook. Is it your journal?"

"Yes, in a way. I jot down a lot of different thoughts that come to me. Some are journal related, others have to do with poetry, song lyrics, or my photography."

"Oh, wow. You write a lot! And you're a photographer?!"

"Yes. Freelance." I responded casually.

"Have any of your poems been published?"

"Not yet. Maybe someday."

"How about your songs? Has anyone recorded them?"

"Same. I've been writing for a while but I'm really just trying to improve my craft at this point."

"I hope you don't mind me asking all of these questions."

"Not at all. It's nice to talk with someone."

"So, another question ... where are you from?"

"The San Francisco Bay Area. And you?"

"St. Louis."

"Wow! You're a *long* way from home! What brought you out here?"

"I was in Portland for a convention and added a couple of vacation days into my schedule so I could go skiing. I heard that Mt. Hood was a great place to go and I thought I'd check it out."

"I'm glad you did."

She blushed and was about to respond when our waiter arrived with our dinners.

The next couple of hours seemed to just fly by. We talked and laughed about a variety of things, and then it was time to leave. I tipped our waiter and Linda insisted on paying half, but I refused.

"May I at least pay for your dinner since you were so kind to join me?"

"No, that's okay, but thank you."

She smiled that same shy smile that had caught my attention earlier that evening.

As we left the restaurant I wondered what might happen next when I noticed the towering stone hearth nearby. I asked her if she'd like to sit near the warm fire and chat a while longer and she nodded.

"Yes, that would be nice."

I also noticed that some people sitting nearby were drinking something in tall mugs. 'Hot chocolate, perhaps?' Moments later I saw a waitress come out of the restaurant and deliver two mugs to a couple sitting nearby. I caught her attention and asked if she was serving hot chocolate and she replied she was. I looked at Linda and she nodded, so I ordered two mugs for us. When they arrived a few minutes later Linda insisted on paying for them and this time I didn't argue.

"Thank you."

"Absolutely! You've been so generous that I finally found a way to partially repay you!"

"Oh, you didn't have to –"

"Maybe not, but I wanted to." We shared another smile.

"Thank you."

We continued our dinner conversation and for the next hour or so kept warm by the fire, sipping our hot chocolate.

It was getting late and Linda said she'd better get to her room and get some sleep because she needed to drive back to Portland in the morning to catch her flight home. I offered to walk her to her room and she accepted.

Approaching her room she thanked me again for the evening.

"It was my pleasure."

"Good luck with your writing and photography."

"Thank you, and I hope you have a safe trip home."

"Thanks, I'm sure it will be just fine."

We said good night as she put her key in the door, and I headed to my car where, in the middle of the night, and while listening to music on the radio, I wrote *Timberline*. When I was finished I wrote another copy. As I was approaching the Lodge early in the morning in anticipation of getting some great shots of the sunrise, I went into the Lodge, walked to Linda's room, and slipped her copy under the door.

Later that morning I headed out for new adventures, exploring the Columbia River Gorge, making a few stops along the way to take more photos, and wanting so desperately to head north into Washington to visit my close friend, Dave, whom I hadn't seen in a few years. I looked at my wallet, counted my depleting funds, and reluctantly had to pass.

After exploring several parts of Portland and stopping for a light dinner I began my journey home.

# SOFTLY (p. 52)

**WHEN YOU'RE AFRAID TO SAY** "I love you" because it might feel too soon in a relationship you write a poem. At least, that's what I did.

I had known the young lady I was dating for a few years, but various circumstances kept us from actually getting together. When she unexpectedly came back into my life, and I was available, I wasted no time to ask her out. The look in her eyes and the smile on her lips spoke volumes even before I heard her say "Yes!"

Our first date was wonderful! It began with laughter and great conversation, and ended (all *too* soon!) with a very special kiss. Her perfume entranced me. Her eyes and her smile were warm and friendly (they were what had attracted me to her when we first met). It just seemed like we fit together so … naturally.

After dropping her off that night I didn't go straight back to my apartment. Instead, I drove out to a marina, and listened to the waves softly splashing over the rocks of the breakwater. After a while I got out and leaned against the hood of my car and felt the cool, evening breeze coming off the bay blowing across my face and through my hair.

Was this the start of something I had been hoping and praying for for such a long time? Only time would tell. It sure felt wonderful! When I returned to my apartment an hour later I sat down to write in my journal, but this poem came out instead.

# LOVE, 2 (p. 57)

**I WAS SITTING AT MY** desk one evening, my desk lamp was the only light on in the room. I was supposed to be studying for one of my college classes, but I just couldn't concentrate. I was struggling with my emotions, because the young lady I was dating at the time didn't seem to be as committed to our relationship as I was.

I rarely discussed my personal life with my parents. It wasn't that I wouldn't or couldn't, it was just that it rarely came up in conversation between the three of us, at least not much more than the usual, "How are things going?" I knew they cared, and they could always tell how things were *really* going by my mood.

On this one particular night, though, my Dad was walking past my bedroom, noticed that I was just sitting at my desk looking rather down, and stopped at my door.

"Everything okay, son?"

"No, not really." I replied.

"Is it Debbie?"

"Yes."

"Not going well?"

I sighed heavily, "No. I just wish ..." but just left my thought hanging.

My Dad let the silence linger for a few moments and then offered one of the wisest things he ever said to me.

"Love doesn't hit everybody at the same rate of speed."

I looked at him, pondering what he had just said.

"Thanks, Dad." I replied, the emotional pain slightly lifting from my heart. "I appreciate that."

He nodded. "Anytime, son."

As he walked away I continued to ponder what he had just shared with me, and I began to realize how truly profound those few words were. I wrote a few notes in my journal, and then went out to the family room where my Dad was watching TV, sat down on a chair near him, and thanked him again, but this time with much more gratitude.

"Sure, son. I just hope it helps."

"It does. A lot!"

I think we've all faced times in our lives when a relationship we're in just isn't going the way we wish it would. We can't force it, we just have to let it develop as it will, *if* it's supposed to develop at all.

## JULIET  (p. 59)

"**AH, FAIR JULIET! 'TWAS BUT** the briefest time I spent with thee. Return, if thou wilt, and fulfill my dreams!"

I mentioned earlier about how some of my poems were inspired by photographs I had seen, but this one was actually inspired by a photograph I had taken while on a freelance assignment on the campus of UC Berkeley in 1977.

Imagine, if you will, walking across the campus, seeing the coeds dressed in their usual fashion of jeans, sandals, and t-shirts, either plain or emblazoned with one form of message or another. Okay, do you have that image firmly emblazoned in your mind's eye?

Now imagine, seeing a young lady walking across the campus in this stunning gown straight out of the Elizabethan era, as if she were preparing to either attend a grand ball or to appear in a Shakespearean play!! Needless to say, I was stunned!

I raised my camera, focused my lens from a distance, and then followed her every move, taking shot after shot, as she came closer and closer with this most wonderful look of joy on her face.

As it turned out I was in the perfect place to capture this moment, because a young man passed by close to me on my right and her smile seemed to be just for him! It was glorious! I was able to overhear a bit of their conversation and she, indeed, was appearing in a Shakespearean play on campus, and she was dressed that way in her effort to help promote the play! As they parted ways I, too, wrapped up my assignment and headed home.

After arriving home later that afternoon I headed to my darkroom to develop the photos, and after dinner I had the chance to look over everything I'd shot. The photos of this young lady really stood out. One photo, in particular, *really* caught my eye and inspired me to write about it, and I did so in a much different style than I had ever written in before or since.

## TWO HEARTS ARE ONE (p. 60)

**I WROTE THIS POEM FOR** my friends Mike & Kay Robertson not long after they got married. Mike and I have been best friends since third grade, and I had just been his best man (and he was mine less than two years later). After seeing the proofs of the wedding photos I ordered several for myself, including a copy of Mike and Kay sharing a special kiss. They may have wondered at the time why I would want that particular photo, but I knew exactly what I was going to do with it. I later presented them with a 3-panel matted frame with their photo in the middle and this poem placed on each side of it.

## SILHOUETTE (p. 66)

**TRUE STORY.**

It was the summer between my junior and senior year of high school. I was in Europe for six weeks on a trip that began with a few nights in London and ended with a few nights in Paris, with stops along the way in Brussels, Cologne, Heidelberg, Stuttgart, Munich, West and East Berlin, Garmisch-Partenkirchen, Lucerne, Zurich, and witnessing an amazing sunrise in the Austrian Alps before traversing the Innsbruck Valley and then up through the Italian Alps to Tyrol.

We visited famous landmarks like Trafalgar Square, Piccadilly Circus, Carnaby Street, Buckingham Palace, took the Underground in London and the Métropolitain in Paris, visited castles throughout the Bavarian region in southern Germany including two of the many commissioned by King Ludwig II of Bavaria - Neuschwanstein and Linderhof – and the amazing Palace of Versailles built by King Louis XIV, also known as the "Sun King". It was a magical time, shared with many friends, and meeting more along the way, including one very special girl from Lincoln, Nebraska.

## THE ONE (p. 79)

**THIS SONG IS DEDICATED TO** my friend, Janet Roberts Mullen, and was written shortly after her incredible husband, Foster, died in a tragic accident near their home. We had been friends for only a short time, but I could sense her horrific grief and all I could do to try to reach out to her at the time was to write this for her in an effort to ease at least some of the pain.

## IF WE EVER LOVE AGAIN (p. 81)

**THE MAIN CHARACTER IN MY** romance novel *The Reunion* is a singer / songwriter in high school and has aspirations of moving to Nashville after college. I began writing *The Reunion* while living in the Nashville area as a songwriter and music publisher. In the midst of developing the storyline I was also inspired to write a few songs that tied in with it. If the book is ever made into a movie, I'll have those songs to pass along to the producers for the soundtrack. *If We Ever Love Again* is one of those songs.

## ETERNALLY (p. 83)

**THIS SONG TAUGHT ME A** hard lesson. Let me explain.

After several years of being away from my writing, as my wife and I were raising our family of five boys, I had decided to revive my songwriting. I was active in the songwriting community in the San Francisco Bay Area and had joined BMI (Broadcast Music, Inc.), one of the performing rights organizations responsible for music publishing, licensing, and paying out royalties. A fellow songwriter from New Jersey reached out to me and asked if I'd like to collaborate on a song with him and I said, "Sure!"

Robert and I chatted on the phone, and he agreed to send me a tape of the music he'd composed and I agreed to write the lyrics. I've always wanted to find a great Burt Bacharach–Hal David type of collaboration and was hoping this would be the one!

He explained to me that the song was for a young, up-and-coming cabaret artist in New York City, and she wanted to sing a special song at her debut. I, of course, was *thrilled* with the prospect of one of my songs hitting the big time!

I received the tape and immediately began the process of listening to the melody over and over, getting a feel for the emotion of the song, and then putting pen to paper. Normally, I would have finished the lyrics within just a few days at the most, but the format of the music was different from what I had been used to, so it took a bit longer. When

I was finished I started his tape and sang my lyrics to myself and was excited, and hoped he would be, too! I gave him a call, told him I was finished, and sent the lyrics to him.

He called me a couple of weeks later, all excited, and said that he had played it for his wife who was in Europe on her own cabaret tour and said, "My wife LOVED the song and told me I had to hold it for her because she wanted to sing it in her own show on Broadway after she returned home in a couple of months!"

Needless to say I was blown away and couldn't wait to get a copy of the final recording she would do in the studio. That was over twenty five years ago ... and I'm still waiting. That's right, I never heard from him again. Oh, trust me, I've called, written letters and emails, sent texts, and anything else I could think of to connect with him again, but nothing has worked.

My *big* mistake occurred because I was still fairly new in the business, and for all I know Robert may have been as well, and neither of us signed a collaborator's agreement so that we could split our royalties 50/50. Without that agreement I have no legs to stand on if I were to pursue any sort of legal action.

Live and learn ... the hard way.

## THE EDGE OF FOREVER AND GOODBYE (p. 87)

**WHILE LIVING AND WORKING IN** Nashville I made lots of wonderful friends in the music industry. It wasn't long before I had a producer, an engineer, and a fun studio from which to work! When I first approached my producer with three new sets of lyrics she went crazy for this one and begged me to let her compose the music for it. I agreed and she was off and running. A few weeks later the music was finished and she played and sang the song for me in the studio and I loved it. We each recorded our own version of it and I was excited when it received a modest amount of air play on the radio.

# A PLACE FOR HER PIANO (p. 90)

**THE IDEA FOR THIS SONG** came from a friend. Holli is an amazingly multi-talented artist (painter) and singer/songwriter based out of Los Angeles. We were kicking around ideas for a song one evening and this one rose right to the top for me. I shared the lyrics with her and she loved them, but she's been so focused on her painting career that we've never recorded the song. "Thanks for the idea, Holli! I hope I've made you proud!"

# ANOTHER LONELY NEW YEAR'S EVE (p. 93)

**THIS SONG IS PARTICULARLY SPECIAL** to me because I wrote it for a very wonderful friend of mine.

Kathy and I had known each other and dated many years ago but had lost contact. We were able to re-new our friendship nearly 40 years later and enjoyed catching up with one another and sharing stories about our families, work, etc.

A few months later, on New Year's Day, I reached out to her to see how she was doing and to see if she'd done anything special the night before. She said her daughter came over for dinner, and afterwards took off to celebrate New Year's Eve with her friends, while Kathy stayed home alone, watching old movies, and enjoying a glass or two of wine before going to bed early.

Later that evening I wrote this song in less than an hour, set it aside overnight to "simmer", then locked it over the next day and didn't need to re-write one single part of it. When I shared it with her she was so surprised and pleased that I had written this song for her.

# RIGHT HERE WAITING (p. 96)

**THIS IS ONE OF MY** *most* favorite songs that I've ever written. It ranks right up there with *Another Lonely New Year's Eve* and *The Edge of Forever and Goodbye* for the visualizations and powerful emotions it evoked as I wrote it, and I *still* cry whenever I read it!

Another reason it's so special to me is how long I struggled to get it just right. Before I ever shared it with my producer I had rewritten it nearly ten times (I usually average six to eight re-writes per song) and I thought I'd finally nailed it. Leave it to my ever wise producer to see that something was missing. She wasn't sure what it was, but she asked me to go back and keep trying.

For the next several days I read it over and over, but nothing new came to me. Then suddenly I had one of those exhilarating "A-HA!" moments and I had perfect clarity!

The problem was that I had written it for a single voice, either male or female, it didn't matter. I immediately jumped into completely rewriting it with enthusiasm, making drastic changes, and when it was done I had a duet that I am *so* proud of, with a male singing the lead and the female as the supporting voice. I'm not ashamed to say that when it was done, and I read it over from the top, I cried because of the deep emotions that rose within me, and it wasn't even from personal experience just a random idea that came to me.

When I shared the new version with my producer she was thrilled! She could hardly wait to compose the music so we could cut a demo and share it with either Garth Brooks and Trisha Yearwood or Lady Antebellum. She had several projects that she and my engineer had scheduled ahead of this song so it had to wait in line … patiently. Sadly, before our dream came to life, she passed away.

One of these days I'm hoping to find another composer to help me bring this song to life.

### *And now ... one more, for good measure!*

## OLD SONGS

**MY MOST FAVORITE LYRICAL CO-WRITER** is my friend James Odle, Jr. He grew up in Houston, Texas and he and his wife, Terry, still live not far from there. We met through a mutual acquaintance and, because of so many similar interests beyond music, we became instant friends. James has a crazy sense of humor and it really shined through in some of the songs we've written together.

Our emails back and forth were filled with memories from our teen years. "Old Songs" was a result of many of those emails, and although it wasn't a collaborative effort, it was still fun to write. And after all you've read of my many broken hearts I thought I could wrap things up with something a bit more light-hearted.

## OLD SONGS

Listened to the radio today
waiting to hear what the DJ'd play.
Then I heard a love song from my past,
oh, how I wish those times would last.

    But living in the past is impossible,
    though I can always pray for a miracle

        Old songs always take me back.
        Fast songs remind me of dancing all night,
        slow songs, ahhhh, romancing all night.
        Yeah, old songs help me to forget,
        no worries, no cares,
        just go back to yesteryear
        and listen to them old songs.

One song always makes me cry
from the night my baby said goodbye.
I can still see her face and her eyes, so green,
and I think, "Uh-oh, here comes that memory."

*Breaking the Stillness*

But I won't stop listening to the radio,
I'll just hold on to my heart and go with the flow,

> Because old songs always take me back.
> Fast songs remind me of dancing all night,
> slow songs, ahhhh, romancing all night.
> Yeah, old songs help me to forget,
> no worries, no cares,
> just go back to yesteryear
> and listen to them old songs.
>
> Yeah, old songs help me to forget,
> no worries, no cares
> just go back to yesteryear
> and listen, yeah, yeah, yeah,
> to them old songs.

# The End
## (Almost)

**There's one final story** I wish to share with you, but it's not about a lyric you've already read earlier in the book. I wanted to share the story first, and then share the lyrics I wrote … well, just because.

Back in 2006 I read a newspaper article written by F.T. Norton for the Nevada Appeal about the wonderful love story of Bart and Evelyn Allen of Carson City, Nevada. At the time of this story it was noted that Bart and Evelyn had met 64 years earlier while picking tomatoes in Kansas. It was love at first sight and they were married just a couple of months later. They raised four amazing children in a home filled with complete love and never a cross word.

Their family always did everything together, from bowling to playing ball, from attending church to being kind and loving neighbors. They all supported each other in their various activities.

In recent years, Bart and Evelyn had both been dealing with ill health. On July 25, 2006 (their 64th anniversary), Bart became ill and was hospitalized. A few days later Evelyn fell ill and she, herself, was hospitalized. Their family all knew it was now just a matter of time.

They were in separate rooms in the hospital when one of their granddaughters asked a doctor if they could possibly put them together in the same room. As the article stated, "It was like the Red Sea parted. Everyone moved out of the way and they moved Grandma into Grandpa's room and pushed their beds together."

Evelyn's hand was placed in Bart's and it was just a matter of minutes before she passed away. Dave, one of their sons, remembers telling his father, "Look, Dad, she's waiting on you. Don't make her wait."

Another quote from the article, "A doctor scrounged up a camera and they took a close-up shot of those clasped hands – the hands that had nurtured children and grandchildren with an undying love for more than six decades."

Eighty minutes later Bart joined his bride.

Oh, how I wish they'd included that photo with the article in the paper, but then again … that's a poignant, private moment for just the family and the hospital staff to have witnessed and to remember forever.

Their love story inspired these lyrics I wrote the evening after reading this article.

# (WE'LL ALWAYS GO THERE) TOGETHER

He met her back in '42
on a Kansas farm in the spring.
They fell in love and it wasn't long
'til he was giving her a ring.

Kids came along one by one,
there was so much joy to share.
He carved a sign to hang above their door
that said, "Love is spoken here."

> "I'll always stand by you
> with a love that's yours forever.
> Wherever the road may lead
> we'll always go there together."

He made a decent livin'
workin' hard for all he was worth.
She always made their loving home
a bit of Heaven here on earth.

All the kids grew up and went on their way,
and started families of their own.
Sharing so much love and joy,
just like they had been shown.

*Jace Carlton*

> "I'll always stand by you
> with a love that's yours forever.
> Wherever the road may lead
> we'll always go there together."

Their beds were pushed together
in the dimly lit hospital room.
After they placed her hand in his
it was clear they'd be going home soon.

She went first and everyone knew
it wouldn't be long till he joined her,
because of the words he wrote in her heart
so many years before.

> "I'll always stand by you
> with a love that's yours forever.
> Wherever the road may lead
> we'll always go there together."

*Breaking the Stillness*

    Sixty four years of fallin' in love
        more every day.
    Sixty four years of a perfect love
        couldn't keep heaven away.
    The angels sang and a light from above
        showed them the way,
    "It won't be long, you're headed home,
        and it's not very far away."

A whispered prayer and a kiss goodbye
from the family they had raised.
They'd never seen a more perfect love
and to Heaven they gave their praise.

    "When our journey's through
    we know we'll join you forever.
    Wherever the road may lead
    we'll always go there together."

# The End

**A**S THIS COMPILATION OF my favorite poems and lyrics comes to a close I have one more poem to share with you. At the very beginning I mentioned how I initially wrote my poems in just rhyme and rhythm before changing to free verse several years later and staying with that style ever since, but this final poem goes back to that ol' rhyme and rhythm one last time. I wrote this poem a few years ago when I began compiling some very special material for a series of inspirational/motivational books based on my website, ChangeYourStars.com. One of those volumes is being designed specifically for children and youth to help them to believe in themselves and their future with hope, excitement, and enthusiasm. This poem will appear in that volume.

*Jace Carlton*

## CHILDHOOD DREAMS

Little girls and little boys
have lots of playful dreams;
Barbie dolls and Tonka trucks
and sailing ships on rolling seas.

They both get lost in make-believe
and hope that someday
there'll be that perfect one
who'll steal their heart away.

But most times children grow up
and lose their faith in dreams;
broken toys and broken hearts
destroy their fantasies.

*Breaking the Stillness*

Once in a while there'll be a child
who doesn't know the meaning
of "No" or "Can't" or "There's no way"
and blows away the ceiling.

The sky's no limit because they can see
life has so much to give.
Their childhood dreams are so much more
because they've discovered how to live.

So little girls and little boys
look up to the stars!
Hold on to hope and then you'll see
who you really are.

Keep believing in your dreams
and know there'll come a day
all your dreams will come true
that you dream today.

# Some Final Thoughts

THANK YOU FOR JOINING me on this journey. For me it began exactly 57 years ago this month. Along the way there have been many friends and loves who have been the reason for the incredible joy and devastating broken hearts I've experienced, and to each of you I offer my deepest love and gratitude. Without the soaring heart and the seemingly endless tears, I would never have experienced what it means to truly love someone. A friend once told me that unless your heart has been filled with so much love that it almost bursts, and then been smashed into a million pieces, you have no idea what it means to truly give all of your heart to someone else.

My love of writing began with short stories and then evolved into poetry and songs. I've lost track of how many talks and speeches, keynote or otherwise, that I've written and given over the years. They, too, began 57 years ago.

I've shared my thoughts on creative writing to all age levels from elementary, junior high, and high schools, to colleges and universities, adult school classes, as well as church youth and adult groups, and even Sunday evening Firesides because there is most definitely a spiritual foundation for all of the creative arts.

I've thought about creating this compilation for many, many years and I believe that now is the perfect time to put everything together. I'm now focusing strictly on writing romance novels, so *Breaking the Stillness* will be my last offering of poems and lyrics. It's a work of love from my heart to yours.

At the beginning of this book I mentioned that I never intended for my work to ever be published, but a few very close friends made the difference and helped me believe in myself and my work.

As I mentioned in my acknowledgements, one of my biggest supporters early on, and to this day, is my friend, Lou Lois. His persistence resulted in the publication of my first book of poetry, *Sounds of Darkness*, in 1976. He was one of the first to buy a copy, and a short time later his sister, Shelley, asked to read it and came across one particular poem that she wanted to use in her upcoming wedding. Needless to say, I was humbled.

I also owe many thanks to Lynette Kranig, Debbie Hightower, Debbie Childree Corro, Cari Clayton, Sue Brown, and Debra Hunter Miller for offering thoughts from a female's perspective. Additionally, their encouragement, support, and belief in me were crucial for me to decide to share my work with the public, then and now.

If there is one thought I might leave you with at this time it would be to follow your heart. Listen to the promptings you receive, take time to ponder them, and believe in yourself.

Farewell! And I'll see you in the pages of my novels!

Jace
April 2020

# About the Author

Jace Carlton has had a diverse career as a freelance writer & photographer, award-winning poet, web designer, author, an Adult Contemporary radio DJ in the San Francisco Bay Area, and twelve years as a popular and award-winning play-by-play football announcer.

He also spent many years as a songwriter, including eight years in Nashville, TN. He wrote predominantly for the Country genre, but also enjoyed occasionally writing for A/C, Pop, R&B, and Smooth Jazz. While in Nashville he also had his own music publishing and artist management company. As a freelance writer he has contributed reviews on new music and singer/songwriters to online publications, and regularly contributed book and concert reviews, along with personal commentary on the music industry, to Nashville's *Songwriter's Connection* e-Zine. He now devotes his time to writing fictional romance novels.

Jace is also the creator of ChangeYourStars.com and its companion motivational / inspirational e-mail messages that have been read by tens of thousands of people all over the world. He is currently writing a new series of books based on the *Change Your Stars!* theme.

*Breaking the Stillness* is a compilation of Jace's first three books of poetry *Sounds of Darkness*, *Rainwater Tapestry* (unpublished), and *Breaking the Stillness* (unpublished), along with several he wrote over the next few years. A few of his favorite lyrics written during his Nashville years are also included.

Originally from the San Francisco Bay Area, Jace and his wife, Kathi, spent many years in the Nashville and Memphis, TN areas, and now call Eagle Mountain, UT home.

Other books written by Jace include his first romance novel, *The Reunion*.

*Coming in the Future*

**Novels**
At First Glance
Second Chance
A Stranger Passing Through
The Last Letter
All of Her Heart
Dancing With a Stranger

# Coming Soon!

**An excerpt from the romantic thriller**

# At First Glance

# Chapter I

## *Tuesday Morning*

**A.J. WAS EXCITED AS HE** prepped for his appointment with The Allison Company! Roger Allison stood alone as the most respected CEO in the high-tech industry. He had groomed his company quite carefully over the years and was serious about an upcoming merger with one of his top competitors. When A.J. received the call the day before from Roger's executive secretary, Sloane, to request this morning's meeting he was surprised and beyond thrilled. Sloane had conducted painstaking research to find just the right consultant for Roger to work with, and A.J. was her first and only choice.

Sloane's compliments about A.J.'s history as a top flight consultant had boosted A.J.'s confidence to a new level. Not that his confidence needed a boost, but if he could just secure this opportunity it would really add a major star to his résumé! He took one final glance in the mirror, tightened his tie a bit more, straightened it, let out a deep sigh to relieve some tension, and headed out the door.

His commute into the city wasn't too bad this time of morning, and it didn't take him long to find a decent space in the parking garage near City Center Plaza. He reached for his portfolio, locked the car, and made his way toward Robertson Tower.

As A.J. walked across the plaza he picked up his pace due to a winter chill that was setting in. As he entered Robertson Tower he spotted the elevators straight ahead. The lobby was nearly empty and a few people were waiting for the next elevator to arrive. A door opened, they rushed in, and A.J. jogged to catch it but the door closed too soon. As the next elevator arrived he stepped in, pushed the button for the 23$^{rd}$ floor, and was alone for a moment until he heard rapid footsteps approaching and a sweet voice calling, "Please hold the door!" A.J. reached forward to hold the door back and a very attractive young lady rushed past him.

"Thank you!" she said, almost out of breath.

"You're welcome," A.J. replied. "What floor?"

"Oh, 23$^{rd}$ please."

"Nice, the same as me!" As A.J. stepped back to his spot in the corner he quickly glanced at the young lady, they shared a brief smile, and just before the door closed all the way a hand blocked it and pushed hard to re-open it. The man who entered quickly hit the button for the 12$^{th}$ floor, took one look at the young lady, smiled and said with a boisterous, overly confident air, "Hi, I'm Ross Stanton Wellington. And you are?"

The young lady fought back a snicker, kept her eyes straight ahead and replied flippantly, "Not interested."

A.J. laughed to himself hoping that neither of them heard him. The young lady glanced up at A.J. and rolled her eyes, making A.J. laugh out loud.

"Something funny, buddy?" Ross asked angrily.

"Well, as a matter of fact …" A.J. replied through a smile, fighting the impulse to laugh again.

"What is it?!" Ross' rudeness was in overdrive.

"Easy guys," the young lady interjected as she moved just a bit closer to A.J. "Let's ease things up a bit, shall we?" She also waved her hand across her face, repulsed by the jerk's repugnant cologne.

"What's *that* supposed to mean? I was just trying to be polite and friendly."

"Not with *that* attitude you weren't," the young lady calmly replied.

Ross didn't know how to respond. Normally pretty women would accept his engaging them in conversation, but this woman wasn't buying it. 'What's *wrong* with *her*?!' Just then he noticed her talking with the other guy.

"Oh, so you'll talk to *him*?"

"What's your problem, buddy?" A.J. asked. "I accidentally bumped her arm and just said 'excuse me' and she responded 'that's okay.' That was it."

Just then the elevator door opened and without making eye contact the young lady motioned toward the door. "I think this is your floor," she stated sweetly, but with a slight sarcastic undertone.

Ross looked up at the lighted floor numeral, muttered something angrily under his breath and rushed out, but not before making one final caustic remark at A.J. and the young lady just as the door was closing. They looked at each other and burst out laughing at how absurd the whole situation had become.

"Can you believe that guy?" the young lady asked.

"No, I can't," A.J. replied, laughing.

"I mean, what a total jerk! And what was that *awful* smell?!"

"Yes, it *was* horrible."

"I just hope I'll never have to smell that *ever* again."

"I'm with you!"

The elevator stopped again and the young lady stepped out with A.J. right behind and they each started to go in different directions. After a few steps they both stopped and turned to look at each other.

"Thanks for the fun ride," the young lady said, and A.J. smiled.

"Sure! It *was* fun!" The young lady smiled back and nodded.

They started to walk off again but A.J. turned and called out to the young lady.

"Excuse me."

"Yes?" she replied with a curious smile.

"This is probably a strange question to ask since we really don't know each other, but ...", A.J. paused and took a deep breath.

"Yes?"

"Would you like to meet me for lunch today?"

Surprised but pleased by the request from the handsome stranger, the young lady caught her breath and smiled. "I'd like that very much, but I already have plans."

"Oh, okay. I just --"

"But ... if you're free tomorrow --"

"YES! I am!"

"Okay," the young lady replied, a bit surprised but excited by A.J.'s quick response. "It's a date!" 'Oh, my gosh! Did I just say that?!'

"Great! There's a new bistro a few blocks away called Maestro's that I've been wanting to check out."

"Sounds like fun!"

"Is 11:30 okay?"

"Yes, that works for me."

"Wonderful." A.J. let out a big sigh. "By the way ... I'm A.J."

"Hi, A.J., I'm Kathryn."

"Okay, Kathryn, I'll see you tomorrow."

"I'll be there!"

They both paused, neither of them wanting to leave. A.J. finally broke the silence. "Well, I better get to my appointment."

"Yes, I better get going, too."

"It was really nice to meet you, Kathryn."

Kathryn smiled broadly. "And it was nice meeting you too, A.J."

Once again it was clear that neither of them wanted this moment to end, but they finally started to turn. A.J. glanced over his shoulder, noticed that Kathryn had done the same, they smiled and casually waved to each other, then finally turned and walked away.

**A Sneak Peek into my future romance novel**

# SECOND CHANCE

**I WASN'T GOING TO DO** this. I was going to hold off. The poem that follows will be in a future book titled *Second Chance*. But something has been nagging at me (perhaps it was my muse, Kiera?), and I felt the need to publish this now, so here it is.

I guess my reasons are three-fold. First, it's a brand new poem I just wrote, so it's not one that I would have already considered for the compilation you've just read.

Second, I already stated in *Some Final Thoughts* that I wouldn't be publishing any more books of my poetry, so I decided to slip this one in at the very last moment before this book goes into publication.

Third, this poem will appear within one of the journals of my main character, Lance Richards, a highly successful businessman who suffers from severe amnesia amidst recovering from injuries he sustained in an earthquake that nearly demolished his office building in San Francisco.

During his long and arduous recovery, Lance's younger sister, Mechele, is a regular visitor. She talks to him and reads to him from a few of his favorite books. One day she decided to bring in one of his journals, hoping that something in it might trigger a memory or two. Anna, Lance's therapy specialist, observes that there's an occasional, ever so slight response, and wonders if Mechele has found a possible key to his recovery.

After one of Mechele's visits, Anna asks to speak with her for just a few minutes. As they're walking along one of the paths not far from Lance's room, Anna asks Mechele about how she thought of reading to Lance.

"I was really sick when I was 14 and missed a lot of school. Lance took a lot of time away from his own studies and personal life to spend time with me. We talked and I loved it when he read to me from my favorite books. After I recovered, he helped me with my homework until I was all caught up. I've always loved him, and I've never forgotten what he sacrificed to spend time with me. I've wished for so long that I could repay him for loving me the way he did. So, I thought, this is my chance!"

"That's wonderful, Mechele!"

"Thanks! I left the books in his room so when I'm not here please feel free to read them to him, if you'd like."

"Oh, thank you! I just might do that. But perhaps I shouldn't read to him from his journal. They're usually very private."

"Oh, I wouldn't hesitate! If he hears something in there that triggers a response, it would be *so* worth it to help speed up his recovery! In fact, he has more journals that I can bring in, so when we finish one, we can go right on with the next one!"

"That's a great idea! Lance is *so* lucky to have you as a sister!"

As Anna was reading to Lance from his journal later that evening, one particular entry caused a lump in her throat, a poem he wrote titled *Missing*.

I wish I could share more with you, but I don't want to spoil the twists and surprises of the storyline.

# MISSING

You missed our first Christmas.
It was so lonely without you.
New Year's Eve came and went
    without a celebration.

You missed Valentine's Day
and the first day of spring,
walks along the beach
    on a balmy summer eve,
horseback riding on dusty trails,
long drives through the mountains
    with the wind blowing through your hair,
and holding each other so very close,
    as we slowly danced for hours under the stars
        to our favorite songs.

Autumn leaves fell,
and then the rain.
Another winter set in.

You missed it all.

Where are you?

www.ingramcontent.com/pod-product-compliance
Lightning Source LLC
Chambersburg PA
CBHW020422010526
44118CB00010B/380